Summary & Study Guide

The Longevity Paradox

Also by Lee Tang

Dual Momentum Trend Trading
Canada's Public Pension System Made Simple
Summary & Study Guide Series:

Brain Maker

The Gene

The Emperor of All Maladies

NeuroTribes

Brain Storms

The End of Diabetes

The End of Heart Disease

ADHD Nation

The Obesity Code

How Not to Die

Mind over Meds

A Crack in Creation

The Gene Machine

The Body Builders

Into the Gary Zone

Fat for Fuel

The Alzheimer's Solution

Healing Arthritis

Rise of the Necrofauna

We Are Our Brains

The Teenage Brain

The Better Brain Solution

The Plant Paradox

The Fountain

Resurrection Science

Sapiens

Homo Deus

The Beautiful Cure

The Diabetes Code

Brain Food

Anticancer Living

The End of Epidemics

The Rise and Fall of the
      Dinosaurs

10% Human

The Mind-Gut Connection

Civilization Microbia

An Elegant Defense

Cancerland

Empty Planet

The Longevity Paradox

Eat to Beat Disease

For a complete list of books by Lee Tang and information about the author, visit LMTPRESS.WORDPRESS.COM.

How can we live longer and still enjoy the physical and mental qualities of being young?

The must-read summary of "The Longevity Paradox: How to Die Young at a Ripe Old Age," by Steven R. Gundry, MD.

Thanks to medical advances, today we are living longer, but not better. As we get older, we develop common ailments like arthritis, Alzheimer's disease, and cancer. As a result, we expect to spend our old age in a state of steady decline.

In *The Longevity Paradox*, Dr. Steven Gundry explains these age-associated diseases were not caused by aging but by the way we live our lives. Our diet, stress, and quality of sleep affect the health of our micro-biome, which plays a role in causing these diseases.

The book outlines a lifestyle plan to prevent these age-associated diseases by improving gut health, which controls how long we live and how young we feel.

Read this book to uncover the secrets of living a happy, healthy, long, and vital life.

This guide includes:

- ❏ *Book Summary*—helps you understand the key concepts.
- ❏ *Online Videos*—covers the concepts in more depth.

Value-added from this guide:

- ❏ Save time
- ❏ Understand key concepts
- ❏ Expand your knowledge

Summary & Study Guide

The Longevity Paradox

How to Die Young at a
Ripe Old Age

Lee Tang

LMT Press
LMTPRESS.WORDPRES.COM

Title: Summary & Study Guide – The Longevity Paradox
Subtitle: How to Die Young at a Ripe Old Age
Author: Lee Tang
Publisher: LMT Press (lmtpress.wordpress.com)

First Edition: August 2019

Issued in print and electronic formats.
ISBN 9781988970264 (ebook)
ISBN 9781095981665 (paperback)
ISBN 9781987065336 (paperback)

Limit of Liability/Disclaimer of Warranty: The publisher and author make no representations or warranties regarding the accuracy or completeness of these contents and disclaim all warranties such as warranties of fitness for a particular purpose. The website addresses in the book were correct at the time going to print. However, the publisher and author are not responsible for the content of third-party websites, which are subject to change.

To my wife, Lillian, who is the source of energy and love for everything I do, and to Andrew and Amanda: watching you grow up has been a privilege.

Important Note About This Guide

This guide is a summary and not a critique/review of the book. The summary may not be organized chapter-wise but summarizes the book's main ideas, viewpoints, and arguments. It is NOT meant to be a replacement, but a supplement to help you understand the book's key ideas and recommendations.

Contents

Introduction

L ife emerged on Earth about 3.8 billion years ago. The first organisms were bacteria and other single-celled organisms. They survived by using volcanic heat to make food from inorganic materials like atmospheric gases and minerals. They thrived on a toxic gas called hydrogen sulfide but would die when exposed to oxygen.

Mitochondria

As oxygen levels in the atmosphere began to rise, some bacteria hopped inside other single-celled organisms that could live in the presence of oxygen. In exchange for food and shelter, the bacteria would generate power for their host cell. This enabled the host cell to evolve into more complex cells like eukaryotes, which make up the cells of algae, fungi, plants, and all animals, including humans. Today, these engulfed bacteria still live in your cells. They are organelles that burn glucose to produce energy for the cell. We call them *mitochondria*, the powerhouses of the cell.

Other bacteria escaped the deadly oxygen by moving into the animals' intestines, which resembled the anaerobic (oxygen-free) environment in which they thrived.

Microbiome

Hundreds of trillions of microbes—bacteria, virus, and yeast—live within your gut. We call this dynamic community of microbes the *microbiota* and the totality of their genes the *microbiome*. Scientists now use the term *holobiome* to include the microbes in your gut, your mouth, your skin, and the surrounding air. So you're not who you think you are. Ninety percent of "your" cells are not human cells.

The results of the Human Genome Project show that complex animals like humans have fewer genes than plants and fleas. This is because they have outsourced most of their functions to their microbiomes. The human genome has 21,000 unique genes, while the human microbiome has 8 million. This means there are 360 times as many bacterial genes as human genes within you. Your longevity depends on having an optimal mix of genes in your microbiome because each of those genes performs a specific function for the human body.

Longevity Paradox

Over the last five decades, innovations like vaccines, antibiotics, and hygiene protocols have extended the life expectancy in the United States from 66.4 years to 76.4 years for men; 73.1 to 81.1 for women.

Perhaps we've ended what modern advances can accomplish. Life expectancy has declined in the last three years! Today we're seeing both a decreasing life span and a reduced health span. Most people now see their health decline at 50. As we get older, we develop common ailments like arthritis, Alzheimer's disease, and cancer. As a result, we expect to spend our old age in a state of steady decline.

We now know that your gut bacteria influence both how long and how well you live. The *Longevity Paradox Program* helps you drive out the bad bacteria and grow the beneficial bacteria. These strategies have helped Dr. Steven Gundry's patients:

❏ Lower their blood pressure and cholesterol markers.

❏ Reduce symptoms of arthritis and other joint issues.

❏ Resolve multiple sclerosis (MS), lupus, and other autoimmune conditions.

❏ Improve heart health.

❏ Slow or reverse the progression of cancer and dementia.

❏ Lose weight and look decades younger.

Online Videos

1. Meet Your Microbiome (https://youtu.be/Ybk7E7SLbWw)

2. How Two Microbes Changed History (https://youtu.be/lhF5G2k45vY)

3. Origin of Mitochondria. The Little Engine That Climbed the Mountain of Evolution (https://youtu.be/2kUXymf8jhY)

Part 1
The Aging Myths

Chapter 1
Ancient Genes Control Your Fate

A 2018 study published in *Nature* revealed that our genes play a minor role in determining our health. Although our genes predetermine some aspects of our health, it is not set in stone as it can be altered by the environment. The makeup of our gut microbiome is a better predictor of health conditions than genetics. Family history is a good predictor of an individual's disease risk because family members share genes, lifestyles, and environments that can influence their health and their risk for disease.

A recent study from the China Institute found that centenarians have the healthy gut microbes of a 30-year-old. In 2017, researchers identified specific families of bacteria that dominated the microbiota of healthy centenarians—*Ruminococcaceae*, *Lachnospiraceae*, and *Bacteroidanceae*. Unfortunately, we lose most of them as we get older.

The gut microbiome plays an important role in your health by helping you regulate many aspects of your health. An imbalance of gut microbes may contribute to weight gain, high blood sugar, high cholesterol, and other disorders. You have a better chance of sharing the same health conditions as your roommate or your spouse than your biological parents because household members share more of their microbiota than individuals from different households.

Gut microbes don't just impact a few conditions. They play a big role in determining how well and how long you live. They can make you fat or thin by controlling the amount of nutrient you extract from your food. When researchers took feces from obese rats and fed them to skinny rats, the skinny rats became fat. The reverse was also true: eating a skinny rat's feces made the fat rats thin.

Gut microbes can also influence your mood. In the 1930s, doctors treated psychiatric patients with severe depression by giving them enemas with fecal matter from people not suffering from depression. The result: they saw a marked improvement in their mood.

In the 1970s, many people suffered from *Clostridium difficile* colitis because broad-spectrum antibiotics had wiped out many microbes in their gut, leaving the bad ones to overrun the colon. The amazing thing is that fecal enemas made with the poop of healthy people cured many of those patients.

Gut Buddies at Work

Our small intestines can digest simple sugars but have problems digesting complex carbohydrates (fibers and starch), lipids, and proteins. Our gut buddies—the beneficial bacteria in our gut—help us digest our food. Without gut microbes, many of the foods we eat would be indigestible. The bacteria in the colon break down the undigested food into nutrients, vitamins, and hormones. Many patients are deficient in certain vitamins, minerals, and proteins because they don't have the bacteria to produce or digest them.

Our gut buddies have other jobs, too. They keep yeast in check and fight against the overgrowth of other harmful microbes. They train immune cells how to distinguish between a friend and a foe so they won't attack the gut buddies and food particles in the gut. They also create the precursors to many important hormones and regulate cellular metabolism by sending chemical messages to the mitochondria inside the cells of our body.

The Sisterhood of Bacteria

As you may recall, mitochondria are engulfed bacteria inside your cells. They have their own DNA separate from the rest of the cell's DNA. You inherited your mitochondrial DNA from your mother. Likewise, your mother populated your gut microbes at birth with her bacteria as you traveled down the birth canal.

Besides generating energy for the cell, mitochondria are also in charge of cellular communication, cell death, and cell growth. That means they play a crucial role in the aging process. Researchers at the University of Alabama found that mice developed wrinkled skin and extensive hair loss after they lost their mitochondrial function. Their smooth skin and thick fur returned after the researchers restored their mitochondrial function.

Your gut buddies and your mitochondria are like sisters, constantly talking to each other. When your mitochondria receive a longevity message from the gut buddies, they respond by working more efficiently and producing more energy. A major component of the *Longevity Paradox* program involves fostering bacteria that send those messages.

Your gut buddies influence every aspect of your health and well-being. If they are happy, they communicate that by producing "feel good" hormones like *serotonin*. They even protect your arteries from harm. If they are hungry or stressed, they'll send an alert about that too, making us feel tired and depressed.

However, this can all change if you drive off the good bugs and let too many bad bugs in. The bad bugs make you crave the foods *they* need —sugars, fats, junk food, and fast food. These foods make you overweight, inflamed, sick, tired, and more prone to heart attacks, autoimmune conditions, muscle problems, Alzheimer's disease, and cancer.

Want to Live Forever?

Naked mole rats have garnered a lot of attention for their extreme longevity—they die because of random events rather than old age. Scientists believe the answer to their longevity lies in what they eat. These rodents live in subterranean tunnels, where they eat roots and tubers. Their gut microbes help break down these indigestible foods into nutrients and compounds that extend their lifespan. Among those compounds is the hydrogen sulfide that their mitochondria lived on. This may explain why naked mole rats can go eighteen minutes without oxygen.

Naked mole rats also have high levels of hyaluronic acid. They got it by eating tubers. Many long-lived people get high amounts of hyaluronic acid from their sweet potato and taro root-based diet.

Researchers found that the microbiota of the naked mole rat was more diverse than that of a wild mouse. It also had an abundance of bacteria called *Mogibacteriaceae*. This bacterial strain is found in humans with extreme longevity (over 105 years old). Naked mole rats also have a low metabolic rate. In times of drought or famine, they can drop their metabolic rate by an additional 25 percent. You will learn to duplicate this key to their longevity on the *Longevity Paradox* program.

Gut Buddy Evolution

Forty million years ago, humans were tree dwellers, eating two-leafed plants such as tree leaves and their fruits. The other animals were grazers who ate single-leafed plants, such as grasses and their seeds.

Over the course of 40 million years, our gut microbes can digest two-leafed plants, but we still have trouble digesting the compounds in single-leafed plants. One such compound is called *lectins*. They are a "sticky protein" that plants produce as a defense against being eaten—to paralyze the insects that ate them. We are a lot bigger and stronger than a little bug, so we rarely experience any immediate problems after eating lectins. But our gut buddies do. Lectins can alter your intestinal flora and interfere with their hormone secretion. When lectins leak through the gut wall into the bloodstream, they can modulate the body's hormonal balance, metabolism, and health. As a result, we become overweight, tired, achy, and sick.

Mice and rats are grain eaters. Their microbiomes have evolved to handle the lectins in grains because they have been eating single-leafed plants and their seeds for millions of years. They have a special enzyme in their gut which breaks down lectins and other grain proteins.

Although humans began cultivating and eating grains and other single-leafed plants about 10,000 years ago, it is not enough for evolution to develop immunological tolerance to a new lectin. And over the last fifty years, our diets have changed more than ever before in history. We now eat far more wheat, corn, other grains, and soybeans than vegetables. Even our vegetables are not as nutritious as before. Modern farming practices have wiped out soil bacteria and dropped the levels of minerals and micronutrients in our vegetables.

Meanwhile, we have compromised our food system by using herbicides, biocides, drugs, fertilizers, and food additives. We have also exposed our holobiome to toxins from personal care products, factory-produced furnitures, and household cleaners.

Gut Buddy Poison

Antibiotics

Broad-spectrum antibiotics were developed in the late 1960s to kill multiple strains of bacteria simultaneously. They have saved and continue to save lives from infectious diseases such as pneumonia and septicemia. However, they also kill most of our gut buddies. Some of those buddies may never return. Studies have shown that every time you take a course of antibiotics, you increase the likelihood of developing Crohn's disease, diabetes, obesity, or asthma later in life.

By altering your intestinal flora, antibiotics cause your body to go into a state of war, increasing fat storage. A single dose of antibiotics given to a child can make him or her obese.

Traditional farmers feed antibiotics to livestock to prevent them from getting sick and to fatten them up for slaughter. You consume those drugs when you consume meat, milk, and other animal products. Even if you've never taken antibiotics, you've likely consumed enough of them to disrupt your microbiome.

Glyphosate

Glyphosate is the main ingredient in the herbicide Roundup. Farmers spread glyphosate on all GMO and many non-GMO crops. Like antibiotics, glyphosate disrupts your microbiome and makes your gut more permeable.

Glyphosate is found in the meat and milk of grain-fed animals, and in crop plants and products made with them. The lectin load and the glyphosate load in grains and beans are a double whammy.

Glyphosate doesn't just kill your gut buddies, it also inhibits them from producing the essential amino acids needed to make the serotonin and thyroid hormones. No wonder a large percentage of our population is taking antidepressants and thyroid medication.

Endocrine Disruptors

Endocrine disruptors are low-dose estrogen-like agents found in most plastics, scented cosmetics, preservatives, sunscreens, and other products. Antibacterial chemicals in hand sanitizers, soaps, deodorants, and toothpaste act like estrogen in the body. These estrogen-like substances interfere with your hormone system.

Your mitochondria regulate cell-death and cellular metabolism based on hormonal messages from your gut buddies. Disruptions to cell-death can stimulate cancerous cells to proliferate. Disruptions to cellular metabolism can lead to metabolic disorders such as obesity, diabetes, reproductive diseases, thyroid problems, and impaired development of the brain and neuroendocrine systems.

Antibacterial chemicals also hinder your body's ability to absorb calcium and promote healthy bone growth, leading to osteoporosis as you age.

Sugars

Studies have shown that fructose, the sugar in fruit, is a mitochondrial poison. Your gut buddies need complex sugar molecules called *polysaccharides* to grow and flourish, but the bad bugs thrive on simple sugars. If you eat too much of anything sweet, your gut buddies will be starved to death while the bad bugs will thrive and multiply. This is one of the main reasons that sugar is such an absolute disaster for health and longevity.

Artificial sweeteners alter the gut microbiome, killing good bacteria and allowing the bad ones to overgrow. A Duke University study showed a single Splenda packet killed 50 percent of normal gut flora.

Any sweet taste, even from natural stevia, stimulates an insulin response that makes you want more. Instead of helping you lose weight, artificial sweeteners cause you to gain weight.

Online Videos

1. How Bacteria Rule Over Your Body – The Microbiome (https://youtu.be/VzPD009qTN4)

2. The Naked Mole-Rat (https://youtu.be/wyx6jcp9zfQ)

3. The Antibiotic Apocalypse Explained (https://youtu.be/xZbcwi7SfZE)

4. GMOs, Glyphosate & Gut Health (https://youtu.be/jWgnkgYtqnw)

5. Top 5 Worst Endocrine Disruptors For Your Gut (https://youtu.be/Pg8urjz09cc)

6. How the food you eat affects your gut (https://youtu.be/1sISguPDlhY)

7. The effects of sugar on your gut bacteria (https://youtu.be/xlldV0_PWdo)

Chapter 2
Protect and Defend

I n the last chapter, we learned that having the right bacterial population in your gut is essential to prevent disease and live a long and joyful life. But this is only half of the equation. The second half is making sure they stay on their side of the gut wall.

Leaky Gut

The gut wall is protected by a single layer of mucosal cells that allows nutrients but prevents large food molecules, bacteria, toxins, and other foreign particles from entering the body. When the gut wall is damaged, it leads to a condition known as *leaky gut* or increased *intestinal permeability*. Large food molecules, toxins, and gut microbes can pass through the gut lining into the bloodstream. When the immune system encounters these antigens, it responds by producing molecules called *cytokines* that can cause local inflammation that leads to inflammatory bowel disease or acute gastroenteritis.

What can damage your gut wall, inciting constant inflammatory attacks by the immune cells? There are two culprits—lipopolysaccharides and lectins.

Lipopolysaccharides

People eating a diet high in animal fat have lots of gram-negative bacteria in their gut. As these bacteria divide and die, they leave behind fragments of their cell wall containing large molecules called lipopolysaccharides (LPS). LPSs can hitch a ride on specialized saturated fat-carrying molecules called chylomicrons to pass through the gut wall even if the gut is not leaky. High levels of LPS in the gut can increase the gut's permeability.

Lectins

Lectins are the "sticky protein" that plants produce as a defense against being eaten. Their "stickiness" makes them attached to the gut lining, where they are bound and trapped by the mucus in the intestinal barrier. If your diet is high in lectin, all the mucus in the gut barrier will be used to bind and trap the lectins. Without mucus to trap them, the lectins will bind with receptors along the gut lining and produce a compound called *zonulin*, which breaks the tight junctions that hold together your gut wall. That's why excessive lectin intake causes digestive distress. Repeated exposure to lectins may eventually damage the gut wall.

Aging and Autoimmunity

Aging is characterized by chronic, low-grade inflammation, which scientists call *inflammaging*. Inflammaging is a symptom and not the cause of aging. Aging results from an imbalance of the gut microbiota, along with a leaky gut that allows bacteria and other particles to pass through the gut wall into the body.

If the "bad guy" that breaches your intestinal lining is dangerous, inflammation can save your life. When you have an injury, inflammation can help you heal. But when inflammation occurs constantly for prolonged periods of time, the result is chronic inflammation, which is the ultimate cause of all diseases of aging.

When LPSs slip past the border, our immune cells cannot tell the difference between them and living bacteria. They assume that LPSs are the real thing and start an immune response.

Lectins have a molecular pattern similar to that of LPSs. So when they cross the border, they trigger the same immune response from the immune cells. But it gets worse. Their "stickiness" makes them bound to the tissues on many of our important organs. The immune cells not only attack the lectins but also the body tissues bound to the lectins. This "friendly fire" is the root of all autoimmune diseases.

Studies have shown that abnormal bacteria entering the brain from the nose and sinuses can cause *Parkinson's disease*. Other studies have implicated bacteria and other microbes as causing atherosclerosis. A 2018 study showed that bad bacteria entering the body through a leaky gut might be an immune trigger for an autoimmune disorder called *lupus*. The "friendly fire" from our immune system has caused these autoimmune conditions.

Space Invaders

LPSs and lectins aren't the only molecules that cause intestinal permeability. Other molecules that can damage the gut wall include:

NASIDs

Nonsteroidal anti-inflammatory drugs (NSAIDs) were introduced in the early 1970s as an alternative to aspirin, which can cause damage to the stomach lining. These drugs include ibuprofen, Naprosyn, Aleve, Advil, Celbrex and Mobic. We now know that NSAIDs are no better than aspirin. They can cause damage to the mucosal barrier in both the small intestine and the colon. As a result, foreign particles can flood into your body, producing inflammation and more pain. The pain prompts you to swallow another NSAID, promoting a vicious cycle of pain and inflammation.

Proton Pump Inhibitors and Stomach Acid Reducers

Proton pump inhibitors and other stomach acid reducers neutralize stomach acids. These drugs include Zantac, Prilosec, Nexium, and Protonix.

You need stomach acids to kill off most of the bad bugs you swallow before they make it to your gut. Without enough of it, bad bugs can take over. That's why regular users of acid blockers are three times more likely to get pneumonia than those who don't use them.

Stomach acid reduces as food moves along the intestines. With no stomach acids to keep them in their place, bacteria can crawl from the colon into your small intestine, where they disrupt the gut barrier. This can lead to *small intestinal bacterial overgrowth*, a condition associated with an increased risk of dementia.

Stomach acid is so important to protect your gut barrier that researchers use baking soda to treat autoimmune diseases such as rheumatoid arthritis. Baking soda stimulates the stomach to produce more stomach acid, which helps keep the gut bacteria where they belong and prevent inflammation—therefore helps to reverse autoimmune disease.

Proton pump inhibitors (PPIs) do more than neutralizing the acids. They paralyze the proton pumps needed by your mitochondria to generate energy. So, every time you swallow a PPI, you prevent your mitochondria from producing energy. A 2017 long-range study found a significant association between cumulative PPI use and the risk of dementia. Other studies have linked the use of PPIs to chronic kidney disease.

These diseases are all caused by mitochondrial dysfunction. That's why the FDA issued warnings on their use.

We need stomach acids to break down dietary protein into amino acids before our body can absorb them. That's why people taking these drugs are also likely to be protein malnourished. This is not because they aren't eating enough protein. Rather, it is because they have no stomach acids to break it down into amino acids.

If you have horrible heartburn or gastroesophageal reflux disease (GERD), don't use PPIs. Use Tums and Rolaids.

And You Thought Gluten Was Bad

Though most lectins and gluten are too large to get through the gut wall unless it's already leaky, a lectin called *wheat germ agglutinin (WGA)* is so small that it doesn't need a leaky gut to pass through the gut wall to cause trouble. WGA is found in whole-wheat products. Besides causing inflammation, WGA also causes other problems in the body because of its ability to mimic *insulin.*

Insulin is a hormone secreted by the pancreas to regulate the amount of sugar (glucose) in your blood. It does so by pushing the excess glucose into your cells for use as energy. When there is more glucose available than your muscles need, insulin tells fat cells to store the glucose as fat. Once the glucose is ushered inside, the insulin separates from the docking ports so the cells are ready to receive the next hormonal signal.

WGA mimics insulin in docking on cell membranes. But unlike insulin, it doesn't let go. This blocks insulin from docking at the port. It also causes fat cells to continue ushering in more and more sugar to store as fat. As a result, your mitochondria can't get the glucose they need to create energy. Without energy, your cells die. Many people assume that muscle wasting is a normal part of aging, but that is not the case. This insulin mimicry is the main cause of muscle wasting because muscle cells die when they cannot get glucose for energy.

Worst of all, the WGA locks into the docking ports of nerve cells, starving them of energy, too. The brain responds by demanding that you eat more food. But the sugar you eat will just continue to go straight into your fat cells because the WGA has blocked insulin from all your cells. No matter how much you eat, your muscles and brain cells will starve and your fat cells will feast. Over time, this can cause brain cells and peripheral nerves to die, resulting in dementia, Parkinson's disease, and peripheral neuropathy.

Only the Strong Survive

Hormesis is a favorable response from an organism to a low dose of stress that would be harmful in larger doses. In laboratories, mice exposed to low levels of radiation lived 30 percent longer than their unexposed siblings. Other experiments using environmental stressors such as heat, cold, lack of nutrients, ultraviolet light, and toxins all came to the same surprising conclusion: In the right dose, these potentially lethal factors can promote health.

Alcohol is another example of a hormetic stressor. A study has showed that people who drank an average of two small servings of alcohol a day lived longer and had lower rates of heart disease than those who abstained or over-indulged.

We will take advantage of a hormetic stressor called *calorie restriction* in the *Longevity Paradox* program. Studies have shown calorie restriction extends the life span of all creatures. In 2018, the results of a ten-year study showed that calorie restriction extends the lifespan of a primate— a gray mouse lemur that shares many physiological similarities with humans. In the study, calorie-restriction extended the lifespan of lemurs by 50 percent, and so did their health span. The aged lemurs had the same motor abilities and cognitive performance as much younger animals, without suffering from age-associated diseases such as cancer or diabetes.

When you restrict calories, these things will happen:

- ❑ **Less inflammation and disease**. When you restrict calories, you decrease bacterial growth. This means fewer LPSs. Eating less means you also reduce the amount of lectin intake. So calorie restriction decreases the amount of LPSs, lectins, and bacteria crossing the gut wall. Calorie restriction also improves gut wall function by stimulating *autophagy* in the gut to get rid of weak or dysfunctional parts. The result is a longer, healthier life.

- ❑ **More efficient in producing energy**. When your cells think food is scarce, they pack themselves with mitochondria, which produces more energy with less food. They do this by growing more mitochondria in a process called *mitogenesis*.

- ❑ **Increase gut integrity**. Studies have shown that calorie restriction increases the abundance of *Akkermansia muciniphila* in the gut. *A. muciniphila* is a family of bacteria living in the mucus layer and feed on the mucus lining. When they eat the mucus, they release chemicals that stimulate the production of more mucus. The more mucus you have, the thicker your wall of protection from invaders.

Having an abundance of *A.muncinpilia* is associated with a lower risk of obesity, diabetes, and inflammation. When researchers fed *A. muciniphila* bacteria to fat mice, the mice lost weight and showed a decrease in blood sugar levels. This suggests that these mucus-loving gut buddies can help prevent type 2 diabetes. It turns out that the popular anti-diabetes drug *metformin* works by changing the gut microbiota, leading to a higher relative abundance of *A. muciniphila bacteria*.

The problem is that your population of this important gut buddy declines with age. Drinking a fermented green tea called *pu-erh* can promote the growth of *A. muciniphila* bacteria. Practicing calorie restriction can increase your *A. muciniphila* population and strengthen your gut barrier.

Stem Cells and Longevity

Stem cells are cells that can become any cell type when they divide and multiply. You can regenerate aging tissues by using stem cells from the body.

As we age, our stem cells lose their ability to regenerate. Temporary stressing your cells can activate a switch that recruits stem cells from all over your body to regenerate. Studies have shown that after fasting for 24 hours, the cells of mice use fat for fuel instead of glucose. We call this process *ketosis*. Ketosis creates stress in the body and signals stem cells to regenerate.

Dr. Valter Longo at the University of Southern California found that stem cells of people undergoing a calorie-restricted diet or fasting have shifted from a dormant to a self-renewal state. Longo also found that fasting triggered autophagy in immune cells. As old and damaged immune cells died, stem cells swarmed in and differentiated themselves into healthy new immune calls. These findings are promising because having healthy immune cells is a pillar of youthful longevity

On the surface of your intestines are millions of tiny hairlike projections called *microvilli*. At the base of the microvilli are crypts, and living inside these crypts are bacteria and stem cells. These crypts are safe harbors for some key gut buddies. When your body needs more stem cells to repair your gut wall or other parts of your body, the gut buddies in the crypts activate the stem cells in the crypts. This causes stem cells to proliferate and migrate up to the microvilli to repopulate the gut lining.

Another signal that activates the stem cells in your gut is vitamin D_3. Without adequate levels of this essential vitamin, the stem cells remain dormant, even when your gut lining is being degraded. If the lining degrades too much, it can cause malnutrition. In one study, researchers gave malnourished children high doses of the vitamin D_3 (200,000 IU a day) to help with nutrient absorption. The children all gained weight despite not consuming any more calories. With a rejuvenated gut wall, they could absorb the nutrition in the food they ate.

Telomeres are long, repetitive sequences of DNA at the tips of our chromosomes to protect them from harm during cellular divisions. Every time a cell divides, the telomere shortens. A shortened telomere offers less protection against DNA damage. Such damage can lead to diseases like cancer and Alzheimer's. When the telomeres are exhausted, cellular division stops and the cell dies.

Telomeres within an organism can have different lengths. The stem cells living in the crypts have the longest telomeres. Humans with the highest levels of vitamin D_3 in their blood have the longest telomeres and vice versa. So we better get lots of vitamin D. Studies have shown that the average person needs 9,600 IU a day. People can consume 40,000 IU a day without producing toxicity.

The Cyclical Nature of Longevity

In a study of hunter-gatherers, researchers found striking differences in their gut microbiomes among seasons. Specific types of bacteria grew and flourished in their guts based on which foods were available to them. People living in a modern urban setting who had access to any food at any time had no such variability.

The microbiome of chimpanzees and gorillas, too, fluctuates with seasonal rainfall patterns and diet. Spring and summer are periods of growth and reproduction, calling for a higher energy intake. Fall and winter are times of regression and retrenchment, calling for a lower energy intake. But in our modern society, we live in a 365-day growth cycle with abundant calories and no natural opportunity to reset. As a result, our gut buddies population stays the same all year long.

Part of eating for longevity means reestablishing our connection to this all-important cycle. That means changing the foods and periodically limiting the number of calories you eat. During times of food scarcity, our mitochondria kill off any cells that are odd, inefficient, dysfunctional or weak. It is also during times of scarcity that we use our fat stores. We store glucose and excess protein such as glycogen in our muscles and liver, and use that glycogen until more food is available. If we use up all of our glycogen before we get more food, our body converts fat into *ketones* for the mitochondria to use as fuel. Our mitochondria prefer fat as a fuel source because it takes less effort to burn fat than glucose. But our body cannot manufacture ketones in times of abundance when insulin levels are high.

During times of growth and food abundance, our body stores the excess sugar and protein in our food as fat for use during a future famine. But if you eat more sugar and protein before that famine hits, your pancreas will keep releasing insulin, trying to get that sugar out of your bloodstream and into your cells. Over time, this leads to weight gain, type 2 diabetes, a shortened life span, and a reduced health span. Even more distressing is that excess sugar in the bloodstream is the ideal food source for cancer cells, which can reproduce during this constant growth cycle.

Besides the seasonal cycle, the day/night cycle is also a key factor in longevity and health span. All animals have a 24-hour *circadian rhythm* based on periods of darkness and light. The circadian rhythms of sleep are essential for activating longevity. Animals exposed to shortened or lengthened periods of daylight have shorter life spans. In a 2012 study, when researchers restricted people to five hours of sleep for four nights, they developed insulin resistance.

Humans and many other animals have a pair of neuron clusters within the brain called the *suprachiasmatic nucleus* (SCN), which receive light input from the retina. Both calorie restriction and sleep activate a gene called *SIRT1* that controls the SCN. Studies have shown that blocking the SIRT1 gene activity in young mice impaired their circadian rhythm control and accelerated aging. Eating shuts off the SIRT1 gene. A deficiency of the SIRT1 protein interferes with your ability to sleep. Supplements of sleep hormone melatonin enhance the production of the SIRT1 protein.

Your body is part of an orchestrated dance between periods of sleep and wakefulness, eating and fasting. By prolonging the period between waking and eating, we can extend our health span by continuing to activate the SIRT1 gene.

Strengthening the Gate

Besides melatonin, your gut buddies produce other important hormonal signals that help offset the 365-day growth cycle and help strengthen the gut wall.

Butyrate

Butyrate is a short-chain fatty acid produced by certain gut buddies that feed on fibers. The more prebiotics you eat, the more butyrate your gut buddies will produce. Butyrate produces ketones in the liver, which your mitochondria love. It improves mitochondrial function, modulates fat and glucose metabolism in the mitochondria, and has anti-obesity and antidiabetic effects. Butyrate can, therefore, help counteract some of the negative effects of living in a 365-day growth cycle. Butyrate also protects you from cancer by inhibiting cancer cell growth. Studies have shown that butyrate promotes brain health by increasing mitochondrial activity in the brain. When mice with advanced Alzheimer's disease were given butyrate, it significantly enhanced their learning abilities.

Polyamines

Polyamines is another organic compound produced by the gut buddies that help protect the gut wall. They play an important role in cell growth, differentiation, and survival. In addition to protecting the gut wall, polyamines have strong anti-inflammatory properties, promote autophagy, regulate brain function, and have been shown to promote longevity in many animals.

Studies have shown that higher levels of polyamines are linked to increased autophagy and longevity. In one study, mice given supplements for polyamine-producing gut bacteria showed suppressed inflammation, improved longevity, and protection from age-induced memory impairment. In another study, rodents given supplements for polyamines had a 25-percent increase in lifespan. Even rodents that were fed polyamines late in life experienced a 10-percent lifespan increase. The researchers credited this to polyamine's role in stimulating cell autophagy, which kills off weak and abnormal cells and strengthens the overall organism.

Sources of Polyamines:
- ❏ Shellfish such as squid, oysters, crabs, and scallops
- ❏ Fermented foods such as sauerkraut
- ❏ Cruciferous vegetables
- ❏ Leafy greens
- ❏ Mushrooms
- ❏ Matcha green tea

❑ Nuts and seeds, including hazelnuts, walnuts and pistachios
❑ Chicken liver
❑ Aged cheeses
❑ Lentils

Polyphenols

Polyphenols are plant compounds that nourish gut buddies and stimulate beneficial processes such as autophagy. The best-known polyphenol is *resveratrol*, found in grapes, red wine, and berries. That's why red wine is protective against heart disease. Resveratrol stimulates autophagy through a different pathway than polyamines do. So it is essential to get both compounds to make sure that your cells recycle themselves as efficiently as possible.

Your gut lining integrity is essential to your health span and longevity, and it is under attack at all times. On the Longevity Paradox program, you will protect it from all angles by:

❑ Feeding your gut buddies the foods they love. It will help them create compounds that support your mitochondria.
❑ Tricking your body into thinking you're fasting so it will prune your gut buddy population and all of your cells down to the strongest ones.
❑ Thickening your protective, gut lining and mucosal lining to keep invaders out.

Online Videos

1. What's Behind the Leaky Gut (https://youtu.be/3pjaXjmZWpU)

2. Lectins Leaky Gut and Autoimmune Disease (https://youtu.be/5hFZSOyrta0)

3. Leaky gut, LPS, and Disease (https://youtu.be/f0N1Vh0Fv9I)

4. How LPS Causes Endotoxemia And Chronic Illness (https://youtu.be/9Fcy5OvSY8w)

5. Wheat Germ Agglutinin - The Dark Side of Wheat (https://youtu.be/6Bo6pssG6As)

6. How to Use Stem Cells to Expand Your Lifespan (https://youtu.be/9WHhlYby70E)

7. Intermittent Fasting is NOT Starving, its Longevity (https://youtu.be/5HLLcCCr68s)

8. Polyamines (https://youtu.be/iXdLtF2lNQs)

9. Is Melatonin a Good Sleep Remedy? (https://youtu.be/ttvrIK-F68E)

Chapter 3
The Seven Deadly Myths of Aging

MYTH 1: The Mediterranean Diet Promotes Longevity

WE CAN LEARN a lot about how to age successfully from people who live in the *Blue Zones*, the five regions in the world where people live the longest. These places are:

- ❑ Sardinia, Italy
- ❑ Okinawa, Japan
- ❑ Loma Linda, California
- ❑ Nicoya Peninsula, Costa Rica
- ❑ Ikaria, Greece.

Not included in the Blue Zones are two other locations whose residents are long lived: the Kitawans in Papua New Guinea and the residents of Acciaroli, Italy.

Mediterranean Diet

Because two of the Blue Zones are in the Mediterranean, many health gurus advise their followers to follow the Mediterranean diet. Is the Mediterranean diet healthy? Some components are in fact healthy, particularly high intake of vegetables, fruits, legumes, and fish. Grains are a negative component. These folks live long despite eating so many grains, not because of it. Italians have high rates of arthritis, and Sardinians have a high proportion of autoimmune diseases because of their reliance on grains.

Blue Zone Diet

Although there is some overlap among the nutrition patterns in these groups, the populations of the Blue Zones follow different diets.

- ❏ **Loma Linda:** Most Seventh-Day Adventists are vegetarians or vegans, yet 50 percent of their diet is fat. They eat a lot of nuts and soybeans in the form of textured vegetable protein (TVP). TVP is pressure-cooked soy. Pressure-cooking destroys lectins.
- ❏ **Nicoya:** Nicoyan staples include corn tortillas, beans, and rice.
- ❏ **Sardinia:** Sardinians with extreme longevity live in mountainous areas away from the coast, so they eat little fish. Their diet includes goat cheese, goat meat, and bread made from buckwheat and wheat. They consume lots of olive oil.
- ❏ **Ikaria:** Ikarians consume lots of olive oil, herbs like rosemary, and a weed called purslane. They regularly drink wine at breakfast.
- ❏ **Okinawa:** 85 percent of the Okinawan diet is purple sweet potato. They eat very little fat and almost no tofu or rice.
- ❏ **Papua New Guinea:** The Kitavans eat lots of taro root (a carbohydrate) and coconut (a saturated fat).
- ❏ **Acciaroli:** Acciarolesi eat anchovies and lots of rosemary and olive oil. They drink a lot of wine and eat no bread or pasta but love lentils.

So what do these people all have in common? **They don't eat large amounts of animal protein**. The Sardinians eat meat only on Sundays and special occasions. Okinawans eat a plant-based diet that includes only small amounts of pork. Most Seventh-Day Adventists in Loma Linda are vegetarians and vegans. Nicoyans eat meat only once a week. In Ikaria, a family slaughters one animal per year and then eats the meat in small quantities over several months. Kitavans and Acciarolesi eat very little protein, most of it from fish.

In a randomized eight-week human trial, researchers divided people into two groups and put them on a 30 percent calorie-restricted diet. In one group, 30 percent of their calories came from animal protein. In the other group, only 15 percent of their calories came from animal protein. Both groups experienced the same amount of weight loss (15 lbs). However, the blood work of the two groups revealed striking differences. The group that ate less animal protein had lower inflammation markers than the group that ate more animal protein.

The Kitavans and the Okinawans consume large amounts of purple sweet potatoes, taro root, plantains, and yams. These foods are not regular carbohydrates. They are resistant starches. Instead of being quickly converted to glucose, resistant starch passes through your small intestine undigested. So eating large amounts of resistant starch will not raise your blood sugar or insulin levels. This is the key to preventing type 2 diabetes, obesity, and inflammations.

Your gut buddies love resistant starch. When you eat resistant starch, your gut buddies multiply and produce large amounts of short-chain fatty acids—acetate, propionate, and butyrate. These are the ideal fuel source for your mitochondria and the enterocytes that line your gut wall. Resistant starch, therefore, increases your gut buddy population, enhances digestion and nutrient absorption, and fosters the growth of the gut buddies that nurture the mucus layer of your gut.

It is possible that the Kitawans and Okinawans avoid many of the diseases of aging because the increased levels of butyrate help their gut linings remain intact. Many other Blue Zone communities consume foods such as olive oil, purslane, and rosemary that also nourish their gut buddies.

MYTH 2: Animal Protein Is Essential for Strength and Longevity

Animal protein was once the most expensive type of food and is still in most of the Blue Zones. But in the West, it has become inexpensive thanks to government subsidies of corn, soybeans, and other grains used to feed farmed animals, poultry, and fish. This results in overconsumption of animal proteins in many Western societies, leading to an increased rate of type 2 diabetes, obesity, and heart disease.

Dr. Gary Fraser at Loma Linda University has conducted a study of long-lived Seventh-Day Adventists. His results showed that vegans who eat no animal products lived the longest, followed by vegetarians who eat limited amounts of eggs and no dairy products. Vegetarians who eat dairy products come next, and those who occasionally eat chicken or fish came last.

Studies have shown that meat consumption correlates with the risk of developing Alzheimer's disease. When the Japanese transitioned from the traditional Japanese diet to the Western diet, their rate of Alzheimer's disease rose from 1 percent in 1985 to 7 percent in 2008.

A 2018 study of men aged 65 and older showed that higher protein intake had no meaningful health benefits. It did not increase men's lean body mass, muscle performance, physical function, or any other measure of well-being.

The **mTOR** (mammalian target of rapamycin) pathway is a sensor for energy availability within the body. If mTOR senses that there is plenty of energy in your body, it assumes you are in a growth cycle and stimulates the production of a growth hormone called *insulin-like growth factor 1* (IGF-1), which signals your cells to grow. If mTOR senses that there is little energy in the body, it assumes you are in a regression cycle and suppresses the production of IGF-1.

Most of us stimulate mTOR constantly because we always have excess energy in the body for mTOR to sense. So our IGF-1 levels are routinely high. This leads to disease and rapid aging. When cells grow with no period of regression, it paves the way for cancer cells to proliferate. Your cells also never get the signal to recycle old or dysfunctional cells through autophagy. Studies have shown that the lower your IGF-1 level, the longer you live, and the less chance you have of developing cancer.

It turns out that when mTOR scans the body for energy availability, it looks for three amino acids—methionine, cysteine, and isoleucine. These three amino acids are prevalent in animal protein but are deficient in most plant-based proteins. So if you avoid animal protein, you can eat as much plant protein as you want and still trick your body into thinking you're in a regression cycle, so it doesn't produce IGF-1.

Animal studies have shown that avoiding the amino acids most prevalent in animal protein extends lifespan at levels comparable to those that result from calorie restriction. Dr. Longo has shown that doing a five-day modified vegan fast once a month produces the same results in terms of IGF-1 reduction as one month of a traditional calorie-restricted diet. You'll be taking advantage of this "cheat" in the *Longevity Paradox* program to sidestep mTOR and trick your body into thinking you're in a regression cycle.

Don't worry about a protein deficiency if you cut out meat. Nuts and vegetables are good sources of protein. Your protein needs are much lower than you think. Most people require only 0.37 grams of protein per kilogram of body weight. So a 150-pound man needs about 25 grams of protein a day and a 125-pound woman about 21 grams. Your body recycles about 20 grams of its own protein. It is impossible to be protein deficient as long as your gut buddies can digest and help you absorb the protein you eat.

MYTH 3: Growth Hormones Promote Youthfulness and Vitality

In societies where children consume lots of vegetables, they are shorter and begin reproducing later in life than children who eat fewer vegetables. But when they switch to more animal and refined-grain sources of food, their growth rates and stature increase.

One of the major downsides of constant growth is that it promotes early puberty. In 1900, the average age at which a girl began to menstruate was 18. Now they are much younger, some as young as age 8. Early puberty is linked to a greater risk of breast cancer, heart disease, diabetes, and death.

Many studies have shown an inverse relationship between height and longevity. They also revealed a connection between height and cancer. In one study, rapid growth during adolescence resulted in an 80 percent increased risk of cancer fifteen years later. It makes sense since high IGF-1 levels promote cell growth.

Dr. Longo studied a group of people in Ecuador called the Larons, who cannot make IGF-1 because of a genetic defect. These short adults are free from cancer and diabetes, similar to another group with the same syndrome in Brazil. When researchers blocked the IGF-1 receptor in mice, creating the "Laron mice," the mice lived 40 percent longer than normal mice. Restrict the calories these mice consume, and they live even longer, yet giving them the growth hormone abolishes the longevity effect of calorie restriction. This confirms the need to maintain a low level of IGF-1.

MYTH 4: A High Metabolic Rate Is a Sign of Good Health

When mitochondria use oxygen to manufacture energy, they produce a by-product called *reactive oxygen species* (**ROS**), which have the potential to damage cells because of oxidative stress. One prevailing theory is that oxidative stress is the major cause of aging. Yet there is no evidence that people in the Blue Zones experience any less oxidative stress than people living elsewhere. ROSs may have an aging effect, but they're a small piece of the puzzle. The heat generated by a high metabolic rate is a much larger piece.

When a glucose molecule bonds to an amino acid through a process called the *Maillard reaction*, it produces compounds called *advanced glycation end products* (**AGEs**). It has a strong bond and requires heat to catalyze the reaction. When you char a steak on a grill, the crust that forms is made of AGEs. The same thing happens in your brain, in your heart, and even on your skin. The brown "age spots" that show up as you get older result from the Maillard reaction.

In a 365-day growth cycle, glucose, protein, and heat are always present. You are producing AGEs all the time. This metabolic state is one of the underlying causes of aging and degenerative diseases. Consuming animal protein ages you rapidly because it requires a lot of energy to metabolize. Lowering the heat by lowering your metabolic rate is the best way to reduce these reactions and, therefore, the rate at which you age. Since it requires protein, sugar, and heat for this action to occur, cutting down on consumption of sugar and protein is a key component of the *Longevity Paradox* program.

MYTH 5: It's Important to Get Plenty of Iron as You Age

Iron is an essential element for life, but too much is harmful. A study by researchers in Denmark and Sweden found that frequent blood donors live longer than those who donate less often. This is because giving blood reduced the amount of iron in their body.

Iron ages us because it interferes with mitochondrial function. In a 2018 study, researchers at the University of Wyoming found that mice with high iron levels in their mitochondria had oxygen deficits in the mitochondria. They also found that mice with Huntington's disease had overaccumulation of iron in their mitochondria, which causes neurons in the brain to die. These neurons die because your mitochondria cannot access oxygen or produce energy.

Studies have shown that, as a person ages, having increased iron in the blood increases his or her risk of developing Alzheimer's disease. Too much iron in the brain leads to a form of cell death called *ferroptosis*. A study has shown that when Parkinson's patients reduced their iron levels by donating blood, their symptoms are reduced dramatically.

Recall that if you feed your gut buddies prebiotics (fiber), they produce butyrate and use it to signal mitochondria to rev up energy production. Iron accumulation in the mitochondria impairs the line of communication between the gut buddies and the mitochondria. Having healthier gut buddies can help protect you from some of the aging effects of iron. When researchers in Brazil gave rats with high iron levels and signs of memory impairment a single systemic injection of sodium butyrate, their memories improved.

MYTH 6: Saturated Fat Should Not Be Demonized

In the 1950s, Ancel Keys at the University of Minnesota studied the impact of diet on health, longevity, and heart disease. He became well-known for his Seven Countries Study, which showed a correlation between fat consumption and heart disease. The McGovern Commission used Keys' data to produce a government food pyramid that for the first time demonized saturated fats. Thus began the low-fat food craze. Food manufacturers tried to remove the fat from their food products while still making them palatable, so they added sugar. Meanwhile, the government created policies to subsidize the production of corn, wheat, and soybeans and promoted eating whole grain carbohydrates as the cornerstone of a healthy diet. This is the start of the downward spiral we are witnessing in our health and life spans today.

In recent decades, people have criticized Keys for cherry-picking his data. He started out with far more than seven countries in his study, and many people believe that he threw out the data that didn't conform to his hypothesis. The backlash against Keys led many to re-embrace the saturated fat found in animal products and gave rise to the popularity of paleo and ketogenic eating plans.

Recent analyses of his data showed that when they add back data from other countries, there is still a clear connection between animal fat consumption and heart disease. One place where Keys went wrong was he didn't distinguish between animal fat and plant fat. Follow-up studies have shown that while the rate of heart disease increases with the consumption of animal fat, it decreases with the consumption of plant fat.

The best source of fat for longevity comes from plants. Olive oil's main ingredient is oleic acid, a monounsaturated fat. But it is not this fat that protects you against disease. It's the polyphenols in olive oil that signal your cells to stimulate autophagy, which strengthens your gut wall and energizes your mitochondria.

Nuts are also high in monounsaturated and polyunsaturated fat and are protective against heart disease because they contain prebiotic fiber. Eating pistachios, walnuts, and almonds increases your level of butyrate-producing bacteria.

MYTH 7: Milk Does a Body Good

Cow's milk is a daily staple food for many people. While it's still a popular food, recent studies suggest milk may have harmful effects on the body.

About two thousand years ago, a gene mutation in northern European cows changed the protein in their milk from casein A2 to casein A1. During digestion, casein A1 can turn into beta-casomorphin-7 which is associated with type 1 diabetes, heart disease, infant death, autism, and digestive problems. The most common breed of cows worldwide is Holstein, whose milk contains this problematic protein. In addition, conventionally raised livestock and their dairy products contain antibiotics and glyphosate, which disturb your gut microbiome.

If you eat dairy products, opt for products made from goat or sheep milk rather than a cow. The A1 mutation did not affect goats, sheep, and water buffalo, so their milk still contains the healthier casein A2 protein. Most cows in Switzerland, France, and Italy make casein A2.

Stay away from giving milk as a beverage to your children. Cow's milk is loaded with IGF-1. Human milk has far lower amounts of IGF-1.

Online Videos

1. Longevity: Journey into the blue zone (https://youtu.be/Zv0_y1FVW0c)

2. Mediterranean diet, our legacy, our future (https://youtu.be/1Aoj4awQb9g)

3. Animal Protein vs Plant Protein (https://youtu.be/mEZ4D0Q0z7k)

4. Dr. McDougall and Insulin-like Growth Factor 1 (https://youtu.be/mHYFOJBU434)

5. Does a Fast Metabolism Speed Up Aging Metabolic Rate and Longevity (https://youtu.be/nN4wuKe_UIA)

6. Dumping Iron: How Excess Iron Negates Healthy Habits & Causes Age-Related Diseases (https://youtu.be/iMERLuHV3YY)

7. The Story of Fat: Why We Were Wrong About Health (https://youtu.be/5S6-v37nOtY)

8. What Is A2 Milk? (https://youtu.be/GGR8rRwnhYk)

Part 2
Talkin' 'Bout My Regeneration

Chapter 4
Get Younger from the Inside Out

Atherosclerosis was once considered to be a degenerative disease that was an inevitable consequence of aging. Recent research has shown that atherosclerosis is not degenerative or inevitable. It is an autoimmune condition that we can reverse without surgery or medication.

When babies who have received heart transplants grow up, they have plaques all up and down their inflamed coronary arteries, just like those of heart disease patients. The blood vessels of these kids were lined with cells from the heart donor. Their immune systems recognized those cells as foreign and went on the attack, resulting in inflammation of the blood vessels.

Rheumatic heart disease is a complication of rheumatic fever, which develops if a strep throat infection is not treated properly. Bacteria called *beta-hemolytic streptococcus* cause strep throat. Our immune system has immune cells that scan the body for patterns in proteins that look like a foreign pathogen. The cells in your heart valves contain a pattern that looks like that on the *streptococcus* cell wall. So the immune system attacks these cells, destroying the heart valves.

African elephants don't have coronary artery disease in the wild, where they eat only tree leaves. Because of habitat destruction, herds of elephants now eat grass, hay, and grains. Half of these animals now have severe coronary artery disease.

How could a simple change in their diet make them sick? It turns out that both elephants and humans possess a sugar molecule called N-acetylneuraminic acid (*Neu5Ac*) sitting on the lining of blood vessel walls and the gut wall. Lectins have a molecular pattern similar to that of LPSs and are foreign proteins. So when they cross the gut lining and bind to the Neu5Ac molecules sitting on the blood vessels, the immune system launches an attack that ends up attacking the blood vessels themselves.

Most other mammals have a different sugar molecule, called N-gly-colylneuraminic acid (*Neu5Gc*), sitting on the lining of their gut wall and blood vessel walls. Lectins bind to Neu5Ac but cannot bind to Neu5Gc. This explains why captive chimps eating a grain-based diet don't get atherosclerosis or autoimmune disease, but poor grass-eating elephants do.

The animals we eat (cows, pigs, lamb) do not have Neu5Ac on their blood vessel walls. They have Neu5Gc instead. When you eat Neu5Gc, your immune system senses foreign invaders. However, Neu5Gc and Neu5Ac are similar molecules, so the immune system often mistakes them for each other, attacking the Neu5Ac that lines your blood vessel walls. This leads to heart disease.

Studies have shown that people who ate more animal protein were 150 percent more likely to have died from heart disease than those who consumed protein from plant sources. A 2018 study showed that people with an autoimmune condition called inflammatory bowel disease (IBD) were twice as likely to have heart attacks as those without IBD. The data also showed that all autoimmune diseases begin in the gut. When your gut buddies signal for immune cells to attack invaders, the "friendly fires" often lead to autoimmunity.

Cholesterol Is an Innocent Bystander

Back in the early 20th century, a Russian scientist named Nikolai Anichkov put forth the idea that consuming dietary cholesterol causes heart disease. In the 1990s, the China Study showed there were no connections between heart disease, dietary cholesterol, and blood cholesterol. Instead, heart disease was associated with triglyceride levels in the blood.

During a growth cycle when you're eating lots of sugar and protein, your liver converts anything you don't need for immediate fuel into a fat called *triglycerides*. Your body uses the so-called bad cholesterol, low-density lipoproteins (LDLs), to carry triglycerides from the liver to cells throughout your body for storage. Your LDL level increases.

During a regression cycle when you're not eating as much, your triglycerides fall. Your body uses the so-called good cholesterol, high-density lipoprotein (HDL), to pick up the stored fat and bring it back to your liver for reuse. Your HDL level increases.

A recent study found no connection between LDL level and mortality, but a high triglyceride level indicates health problems. The best way to analyze cholesterol data is to look at the ratio of HDL to triglycerides. As a guide, your HDL level should be equal to or higher than your triglyceride level, which signifies that you're recycling more fat than storing. However, because of our 365-day growth cycle, most people have the exact opposite ratio.

Many doctors point to the success of *statin* drugs as proof that cholesterol causes heart disease. Statins work by preventing pattern-scanning immune cells from starting an immune attack when they find anything that looks like a pathogen. This results in less inflammation, less plaque, and less cholesterol. The reduction in LDL cholesterol is just a side effect of the drug, not something that makes it effective in treating heart disease.

Triglycerides Are the Real Enemy

Eating sugar and fruit raises your triglyceride levels. Fructose, the main sugar in fruit, is a toxin that can disrupt mitochondrial function. Your body cannot digest fructose. It sends 70 percent of it to your liver, where it converts the fructose into triglycerides and uric acid. The rest heads to your kidneys, where it poisons your filtering system. When we ate fruit only during the summer, we could handle it in small doses because we then had nine months to detox before the next growth cycle. Eating fruit year-round is extremely aging!

Grains also raise triglyceride levels. People make foie gras by force-feeding whole grains to geese. The geese make so many triglycerides in their livers that they get fatty livers. If you have fatty liver or *nonalcoholic steatohepatitis* (NASH), it's likely that you have eaten too much grain and fruits.

Eating protein also raises triglyceride levels because your body converts any excess protein into sugar. As a result, many people who eat high-protein diets struggle with high triglyceride levels and insulin resistance.

It All Goes Back to the Gut

Most chronic diseases originate in the gut.

Overconsumption of alcohol causes a leaky gut by damaging the gut wall, which allows bad bugs and LPSs to enter the liver, where they trigger inflammation. The scar tissue that signifies cirrhosis is an end-stage sign of this inflammation.

Obese men with fatty liver disease have elevated levels of *zonulin* in their blood. Zonulin breaks the tight junctions between the cells lining your gut, leading to a leaky gut. Specific bad bugs can increase susceptibility to fatty liver disease by stimulating inflammation. The right population of gut buddies can protect you from inflammation and reduce the severity of the disease.

If you have a leaky gut, invaders can stimulate inflammation in any vascular interface. Pulmonary fibrosis is an inflammatory attack on the blood vessels of the lung. You can treat it by fixing the gut.

You can even stop hearing loss by fixing the gut. Researchers found that women who ate plenty of olive oil, vegetables, nuts, and fish lowered their risk of developing hearing loss by 30 percent.

The Cyclical Nature of Cancer

When you eat sugar or protein, your body releases insulin to usher sugar into cells to be used as fuel. If you regularly eat lots of sugar or protein, all your cells will be packed with glucose. The body has to release more and more insulin to usher glucose into the cells. This is the root cause of *insulin resistance*. In people with insulin resistance, their glucose and insulin levels are persistently high. Insulin is another growth hormone that stimulates the cancer cells to grow, and cancer cells thrive on glucose.

The 365-days-a-year growth cycle provides a rich opportunity for cancer cell growth. You must give your body a chance to reset and prune those abnormal cells by regularly but temporarily restricting your energy intake. Many people try to "cheat" the system by cutting back on their sugar consumption and encouraging their mitochondria to use stored fat instead. This process (called *ketosis*) is a more efficient way for your mitochondria to produce energy. However, your mitochondria cannot use stored fat directly. Your body must convert stored fat into *ketones*. This requires an enzyme called *hormone-sensitive lipase* (HSL), which works only when your insulin levels are low. Since sugar and protein raise insulin levels, a high-protein diet prevents your body from making ketones. This is a big problem with many ketogenic diets that promote excessive protein consumption.

Recall that you have a sugar molecule called Neu5Ac lining your blood vessels and your gut wall, while many of the animals you eat have a similar sugar molecule called Neu5Gc. When you eat Neu5Gc, your immune system senses foreign invaders, mistakenly attacking the Neu5Ac that lines your blood vessel walls. As this immune attack is happening, your body produces a hormone called *vascular endothelial growth factor* (VEGF), which attracts blood vessel growth to cancer cells, contributing to cancer growth. The tumor cells also use Neu5Gc to shield them from immune cells so they can go unnoticed.

Studies have shown that human tumors contain large amounts of Neu5Gc, even though our bodies cannot manufacture it. This confirms the link between the consumption of animal protein and the development of cancerous tumors. A recent study found a significant increase in the risk of colon cancer among women who ate red meat.

Mitochondria in cancer cells cannot use ketones to produce energy the way your healthy cells can. Your body produces ketones when insulin and glucose levels are low, while cancer cells thrive on sugar. The mitochondria in cancer cells create energy through an inefficient process of sugar fermentation. As a result, the average cancer cell needs up to eighteen times as much sugar to grow and divide as normal cells. It's therefore easy to starve cancer cells to death. They cannot grow and thrive without lots and lots of sugar.

When you limit sugar and animal protein consumption and trick your body into thinking it is during a regression cycle, you reduce your risk of both cancer and autoimmune disease.

Epithelial cells lining the surfaces of organs can sense malignant cells and remove them. A study showed that when researchers fed mice a high-fat diet to make them obese, they suppressed this defense mechanism for mice and increased their rates of cancer. So a diet high in animal fat promotes cancer growth.

The Best Foods for Fighting Cancer

Exogenous Ketones

Instead of becoming ketogenic (producing our own ketones from body fat stores), we can consume ketones and ketogenic precursors. Several plant fats contain ketogenic fats. Medium-chain triglycerides (found in MCT oil) can be converted to ketones. Solid coconut oil (meaning it is solid below about 70 degrees) contains 65 percent MCTs. Red palm oil contains 50 percent MCTs and is loaded with vitamin E's tocopherols and tocotrienols. Note that palm oil is not red palm oil. Palm oil production is associated with deforestation.

Butyrate is also a source of making ketones. It is present in small quantities in butter. Goat butter, buffalo butter, or ghee are better than regular or even raw or grass-fed cow milk butter because most American dairy products have the casein A1 protein.

When we eat a diet high in sugar, protein, and fat (our Western diet), our high insulin levels block our ability to convert fat stores into ketones. Exogenous ketones are best used as an energy source when you are transitioning from the Western diet over to the *Longevity Paradox* program. However, you don't need them long term. Remember, consuming lots of extra ketones won't help if you're still eating burgers and bagels.

Nuts

Researchers found that cancer patients eating two or more servings of nuts a week had a 42 percent reduced rate of cancer recurrence and a 57 percent reduced rate of death. There were no reductions in cancer recurrence or death in patients who ate peanuts. Peanuts are not nuts. They are legumes loaded with lectins. Peanut lectin promotes colon cancer in animal studies.

Nuts are low in methionine, the amino acid that mTOR is looking for to detect energy availability. So eating nuts signals your body that you are in a regression cycle, which helps you fight cancer. In addition, your butyrate-producing gut buddies love nuts, and your mitochondria can use butyrate as a source of ketogenic fat. So nuts are the perfect cancer-fighting food: they starve cancer cells while supercharging your gut buddies and your mitochondria.

Online Videos

1. Inflammation and Heart Health (https://youtu.be/EFKVGlvpsvQ)

2. Heart autoimmunity (https://youtu.be/zzU-MB-NgY3M)

3. Rheumatic Fever & Heart Disease (https://youtu.be/ivIE8ARRIgM)

4. The Truth About Cholesterol - Does It Cause Heart Disease? (https://youtu.be/0RKrFQ-cKZc)

5. Understanding Triglycerides (https://youtu.be/XZSjw4TbIJk)

6. Cancer Lives On Sugar AND...Something Else (https://youtu.be/rewf0MMhGg8)

7. MCT Oil Benefits | They Are Really Incredible (https://youtu.be/cbDCjIAumOc)

8. Super Food: Walnuts protect against many cancers (https://youtu.be/mjlaL4a9HaU)

Chapter 5
Dance Your Way into Old Age

For years, doctors believed that arthritis was a degenerative disease caused by aging—the older you get, the more wear and tear damage on your joints. Recent research shows that arthritis is caused by systemic inflammation created by an imbalance in your gut microbiota and a leaky gut. It's that inflammation that "wears and tears" your joints, not aging. Studies have shown that feeding probiotics (beneficial bacteria) to arthritic mice reduces their systemic inflammation and slows down the breakdown of cartilage in their arthritic knees.

A leaky gut releases lectins and LPSs into your body. Lectins bind onto the sugar molecules on your joint surface, prompting an immune attack. Those LPSs also get into your joints and incite the same response. The resulting inflammation leads to arthritis. When doctors draw fluid from an arthritic joint, they find LPSs in the fluid.

What Really Causes Wear and Tear

The cells in the cartilage that protects your joints are constantly destroyed and regrown. But this occurs unevenly when the joints are inflamed, resulting in peaks and valleys that make a "bone and bone" joint.

Many arthritic patients take nonsteroidal anti-inflammatory drugs (NSAIDs) to relieve pain and inflammation. The problem is that these drugs damage your gut barrier, letting in more invaders. This becomes a vicious cycle of more pain and inflammation, more drugs, more damage to the gut barrier, more pain and inflammation, and so on.

To break this cycle, you must nourish your gut buddies and heal your gut wall. This will suppress inflammation and enable you to stop taking NSAIDs. One of the critical steps in this process is to remove foods containing WGA from your diet. As you recall, WGA is small enough to slip past the gut barrier. WGA is in all whole wheat and whole-grain products, including pasta, bread, crackers, bulgur (cracked wheat), rye, barley, and brown rice.

Keep Your Bones and Muscles Strong, Healthy, and Hungry

Years of chronic inflammation also cause our bones to deteriorate, resulting in *osteopenia* (invisible bone loss) and *osteoporosis* (a condition in which bones become weak and brittle). This is a health crisis among the elderly. One in two women and one in four men aged 50 and older will break a bone because of osteoporosis.

Chickens at factory farms fed with GMO corn develop osteoporosis. When you consume the meat, you are also consuming the inflammatory feed that will contribute to your own bone deterioration. Studies have shown that postmenopausal women who eat a diet high in nuts, vegetables, and olive oil have a higher bone density and a lower risk of heart disease, diabetes, and cancer.

Invisible muscle loss is the greatest risk to our musculoskeletal systems as we age. On average, a 40-year-old's thighs have half the muscle mass of a teenager. Fat has replaced the other half of the muscle mass, producing an intermingling of fat within the lean muscles. We call this intermingling *marbling*. A cow's marbling comes from its grain-based diet. The same goes for humans.

When you eat sugar (or protein, which is converted into sugar), the glucose level in the blood rises. Insulin pushes glucose into your muscle cells for use as energy. But if you're insulin resistant and/or WGAs are blocking insulin receptors on your muscle cells, your body produces more insulin to convert the extra sugar into fat. Over time, it leads to more fat storage and loss of muscle mass. Eventually, it leads to *sarcopenia*—a severe loss of muscles—in older patients.

Strength-training exercises grow muscle mass. When you exercise your muscles, they get hungry, making it easy for insulin to push glucose into cells. This increases your insulin sensitivity and muscle mass and reduces your fat. But eating lectins and WGA can undo much of the benefit conferred by strength training.

Calorie restrictions and exercise can help turbocharge your cells with more mitochondria. Most older people don't restrict calories or do much strength training. The result is less muscle mass and fewer mitochondria. No matter how old you are, it's never too late to reap the benefits of exercise.

Use It or Lose It

A sedentary lifestyle *causes* us to age! People who continue to exercise well into their ripe old age live longer and stay healthier than those who stop moving and allow their muscles to waste away.

The residents of the Blue Zones walk up and down those hills long into their old age, maintaining muscle mass and dexterity for decades longer than most Americans do. Working against gravity when exercising stresses and strengthens more muscles. Hiking, walking up and down hills and stairs, and doing squats and push-ups are all examples of exercises that force you to work against gravity.

Exercise stimulates both *autophagy* and *unfolded protein response* (UPR). Autophagy is the process in which the cell recycles old and worn-out components. The benefits are stronger the earlier you start exercising. UPR is a similar process in which the cell degrades dysfunctional (misfolded) proteins to restore health.

When left to their own devices, worn-out cellular components and misfolded proteins can cause the cell to become cancerous. Rejuvenating the cells through autophagy and UPR helps keep you young and cancerfree. The benefits of exercise include:

- ❑ **Exercise increases your body's ability to regenerate tissues.** A study has shown that exercise can produce new heart muscle cells in both healthy mice and mice suffering from heart damage.

- ❑ **Regular exercise reduces the risk of Alzheimer's disease.** A recent study showed that a physically fit middle-aged woman is 90 percent less likely to develop Alzheimer's disease. Another study found that exercise improved memory performance and reduced atrophy of the hippocampus, the memory centers of the brain. We also know that exercise that uses the legs stimulates brain cells, keeps you alert and healthy long into old age. Meanwhile, "brain training" apps that claim to help you improve your brain do nothing for working memory or IQ. So skip the games and go out for a walk instead.

- ❑ **Exercise has a powerful effect on the immune system** because it causes you to produce more of the enzymes that support cellular and mitochondrial function.

- ❑ **Exercise changes the microbiome.** Studies have shown that exercise increases the diversity of gut bacteria. One study showed that rats that exercised produced more butyrate than rats that did not. Butyrate protects your gut lining and the preferred fuel for your mitochondria. By bolstering your gut wall and your microbiome, exercise reduces your risk of cancer, arthritis, and heart disease.

❑ **Exercise boosts the feel-good hormones**. A recent report from Harvard Medical School states that regular exercise works like prescription antidepressants for some adults struggling with depression.

Chronic Cardio = Chronic Stress

Exhaustive exercise negates the benefits of moderate exercise. Exhaustive exercise causes oxidative stress by creating free radicals that cause aging. During long-distance runs, so much blood flows to your muscles and away from your gut that you experience ischemia (inadequate blood flow) in the gut. This causes gut permeability, allowing lectins, LPSs, and bacteria to enter your body. This is why your immune system tanks for about two weeks after an endurance run.

Blue Zone residents are all hikers and walkers, not long-distance runners. Running marathons impairs your immune system and causes you to lose muscle mass. Long-distance running causes myocardial fibrosis, which leads to arrhythmias and congestive heart failure. Though temporary stress has positive effects, long-distance running places too much stress on your heart for too long.

Online Videos

1. Rheumatoid arthritis - causes, symptoms, diagnosis, treatment, pathology (https://youtu.be/6ylzE5usu7o)

2. Dr. Mercola Discusses Rheumatoid Arthritis Treatment (https://youtu.be/7L2-uaIQBs0)

3. Osteoporosis: Causes, Symptoms & Treatment (https://youtu.be/fuMaTOFPu4I)

4. Osteopenia: The Warning Sign (https://youtu.be/P5op82RdkW4)

5. Many Benefits of Exercise: Mayo Clinic Radio (https://youtu.be/IASpJA5NPFg)

6. What Too Much Exercise Does To Your Body And Brain (https://youtu.be/jfrlygii0Vw)

7. Jogging Vs. Sprinting (HIIT)- Fat Loss, Muscle Growth (https://youtu.be/0hXRT8uZMqE)

Chapter 6
Remember Your Old Age

As you get older, your brain feels foggy and you're just not as sharp as you used to be. Many people think of these symptoms as a normal part of aging. Recent research shows that you don't need to experience cognitive decline as you age. The cognitive decline that we think of as a normal part of aging is caused by *neuroinflammation*—inflammation in the brain—that damages the neurons. Neuroinflammation starts in the gut. No matter how old you are, you can still make new brain cells, learn new skills, and retain memory by keeping your gut microbes happy.

The Brain in Your Head Is Actually Your Second Brain

We now know that the gut and the brain are intricately connected. This gut-brain communication is hard-wired by the vagus nerve and facilitated by chemical signals carried through the bloodstream. The vagus nerve controls most of your autonomic functions like heart rate, respiratory rate, and digestion. For years, scientists believed the vagus nerve existed for the brain to communicate and give orders to the rest of the body, including the gut. We now know that it is the other way around. There are nine times as much communication going from the gut to the brain as there is going in the opposite direction. Your gut controls the brain in your head, which you might think of as your second brain.

Keep Troops at the Outpost

Neurons are cells within the nervous system that transmit information to other nerve cells, muscle cells, or gland cells. Most neurons have a cell body, an *axon*, and *dendrites*. Axon is the nerve fiber that extends from the cell body to carry messages from the neuron to other neurons. Dendrites extend from the neuron cell body and receive messages from other neurons. *Synapses* are contact points where one neuron communicates with another. Your neurons use these structures to create neural networks. Communication among these networks controls most of your thoughts, actions, and even movements.

Your body uses *glial* or *microglial* cells to protect neurons. When they detect invaders breaching the blood-brain barrier, the glial cells prune away the neuron's dendritic structures to protect against invaders. When this happens often enough, the neuron has no dendritic structures left to communicate with other neurons. As a result, you suffer from memory and cognition problems.

Even worse, once the glial cells have gotten the neuron down to the cell body with no dendritic structures, they crowd around that cell body and protect it so well that even nutrients can't get in. As a result, the neuron dies.

When lectins and LPSs cross the gut barrier, they climb the vagus nerve to the brain and settle in the substantia nigra. The neurons in the substantia nigra are dopamine-producing cells. Dopamine regulates emotions, moods, and muscle movements. When inflammation damages the dopamine-producing neurons in the substantia nigra, the result is Parkinson's disease. *Lewy bodies* found in the brains of Parkinson's patients are dead neurons surrounded by glial cells.

Glutamate is an amino acid that kills off dopamine-producing neurons. Your gut bacteria produce this amino acid from glutamine, which is found in MSG, a flavor enhancer present in many prepared foods. Aspartame (NutraSweet, the pink sweetener packet) also converts to glutamate in your gut. Until recently, it was the preferred sweetener in diet drinks.

Curcumin is an anti-inflammatory polyphenol found in turmeric, a main ingredient of curries. It is one of the few known compounds that can pass through the blood-brain barrier to calm neuroinflammation. Researchers at the UCLA Longevity Center showed that people who took curcumin for eighteen months had significant improvements in their verbal memory, visual memory, and attention span.

Multiple Sclerosis in the Gut

Multiple sclerosis (MS) is an autoimmune disease in which the immune system attacks the myelin—the insulating covers of nerve cells—disrupting the communication between the brain and the rest of the body. We now know that some specific gut buddies produce molecules called *polysaccharides* that regulate the production of myelin. Without enough polysaccharides, the immune system attacks the myelin, resulting in MS. In one study, researchers found that giving mice probiotics containing polysaccharide-producing bacteria helps protect their myelin, making them less vulnerable to MS.

This is promising for many MS patients, as MS is normally treated with drugs that suppress the immune system. Recently, Dr. Terry Wahls demonstrated that diet and lifestyle changes can reverse MS. She reversed her MS by eating nine cups of vegetables a day and removing the majority of lectin-containing foods from her diet.

Wash Your Brain Every Night

For decades, scientists studying Alzheimer's disease have been focusing on a protein called *beta-amyloid* that accumulates in the brains of Alzheimer's patients. They believed that the brain produced the amyloids that killed off neurons and caused Alzheimer's disease. Pharmaceutical companies have developed anti-amyloid drugs that would treat and prevent Alzheimer's. However, all of those drugs have been a dismal failure because amyloids aren't coming from the brain. They're coming from the gut.

If you have a healthy population of gut buddies, you won't make amyloid proteins. Your gut bacteria produce amyloid when their own proteins die or become dysfunctional. Even if they produce amyloids, as long as the amyloids don't make it out of the gut, they'll never cross the blood-brain barrier. Problems occur when the gut barrier becomes permeable. The amyloid molecules can enter the body through the leaky gut and climb the vagus nerve to the brain.

Amyloids don't automatically cause damage when they reach the brain. Scans of many patients with no evidence of Alzheimer's show the presence of amyloid proteins. The body normally washes it out at night. But if they stay, they become self-perpetuating by stimulating the brain to produce more amyloids, which accumulate and contribute to Alzheimer's and other forms of neurodegeneration.

The Brain's Housekeeping System

The *lymphatic system* is a network of tissues and organs that help rid the body of toxins, waste and other unwanted materials. The primary transport is lymph, a clear fluid containing proteins and white blood cells. Lymph flows through the body and drains away any garbage in the spaces between cells. Until recently, no one knew whether a similar process occurred in the brain. People thought the blood-brain barrier kept the lymph from reaching the brain.

Recently, researchers discovered a similar system that allows cerebrospinal fluid to flow through the brain, cleaning out the spaces in between cells. They called it the *glymphatic system*. To make room for the fluid to wash out your brain, your brain cells shrink in size when you are in a deep sleep. This allows the "brain wash" to go twenty times faster than when you are awake. That explains why a good night's sleep is so restorative.

The glymphatic system is the most active during a specific stage of deep sleep that happens early in the sleep cycle. It requires a great deal of blood flow. This means that if you eat before going to bed, your blood will flow to your gut to aid in digestion and cannot reach your brain to help with the brainwash. The solution is to leave as big a gap as possible between your last meal of the day and your bedtime. The minimum time between finishing your last meal and going to sleep should be four hours. To get the full cleansing effects without sacrificing your schedule or sanity, the *Longevity Paradox* program recommends skipping dinner once a week (or more) to make sure your blood can flow to your brain when you get to sleep. You'll also benefit from temporarily stressing your cells with this brief intermittent fast.

Obesity and the Brain

Obesity is a major risk factor for dementia because of its impact on inflammation throughout the body. Researchers at University College London found that obese people were more likely to develop dementia than lean people. Those who had central obesity were the most affected. The Longevity Paradox program helps you lose weight to improve the health of your body and mind.

Eat for Your Brain

Olive oil is the main source of dietary fat in the Mediterranean diet. New studies have suggested using it as a therapy to prevent dementia. Why is olive oil so good for you?

Many studies have looked at the health benefits of olive oil.

❑ **Olive oil a high level of polyphenols**. Your gut buddies convert polyphenols into anti-inflammatory compounds.

❑ **Olive oil suppresses the gut microbes from producing vessel-damaging compounds called TMAOs** from animal proteins. That may explain why it is associated with a reduced risk of Alzheimer's.

❑ **Olive oil stimulates autophagy**, the beneficial cellular recycling process. Studies have shown that mice eating a diet rich in olive oil have higher levels of autophagy.

❑ **Olive oil–consuming mice perform better on memory and learning tests** than their non-olive oil–fed peers. Olive oil-consuming mice also have reduced levels of amyloid plaques in their brains.

❑ **Olive oil reduces your blood sugar levels and helps you lose weight.** Olive oil consumption stimulates the brain stem to produce a hormone called *glucagon-like peptide-1* (GLP-1), which decreases blood sugar levels and helps weight loss and treating type 2 diabetes.

❑ **Olive oil protects your brain from amyloid toxicity.** GLP-1 protects synaptic activity in the brain from the negative effects of any amyloids that don't get washed out at night.

❑ **Olive oil stimulates the growth of new neurons.** Olive oil consumption stimulates the production of *brain-derived neurotrophic factor* (BDNF), a protein that promotes the growth of dendrites and axons and supports their connectivity. BDNF also supports the growth of new neurons, leading to better long-term memory and cognition.

❑ **Olive oil improves your microbiome diversity.** A study showed that monkeys eating a Mediterranean-style diet for two years had a higher microbiome diversity and a better ratio of gut buddies to bad bugs compared to monkeys eating a Western diet.

❑ **Olive oil improves brain health.** Studies have shown that people who ate more olive oil and less fried foods and red meat had half the rate of brain shrinkage for their age group.

Something's Fishy

Consumption of small fish is another component of the Mediterranean diet. Studies have shown that people with the highest fish and long-chain omega-3 fatty acid intakes lived longer and had a lower risk of cardiovascular and respiratory diseases. Women with the highest omega-3 intake had 40 percent less Alzheimer's disease mortality. Note: fried fish consumption didn't produce the same results. So back off on those fish-and-chips!

Studies using brain scans showed that patients with higher omega-3 indexes had increased blood flow in regions of the brain associated with learning, memorizing, and avoiding depression. The Women's Health Initiative Study showed that women with the highest omega-3 intakes had the biggest brains and the biggest memory areas compared to those with the lowest intakes.

The best sources of omega-3s are sardines, herrings, anchovies, and other small fish. The Acciaroli centenarians and the Kitavans: they eat primarily anchovies and other small fish.

Eat Your Greens!

A study at Tufts University showed that eating just one serving of leafy green vegetables per day slowed the rate of cognitive decline by eleven years. This means you can make your brain eleven years younger by eating greens every day.

Your Gut Buddies are Yogis

Unhealthy stress levels affect the gut, promoting a high population of bad microbes and altering gut permeability. Extreme stress leads to bad bugs and a leaky gut.

Your gut buddies produce *norepinephrine*, which increases alertness, focus, and attention. They also produce serotonin, the "feel-good" neurotransmitter that increases feelings of well-being. Other gut buddies produce GABA, which calms neurons and reduces stress. When bad bugs take control of your gut, you will feel more stress because you are getting less of these "feel-good" hormones. So it goes both ways. Stress alters the gut biome, and changes to the gut biome create feelings of stress.

The primary benefit of meditation/yoga is a stress reduction, which creates positive changes in your microbiome that provide health benefits.

- ❏ **Yoga/meditation increases telomerase activity.** The length of the telomeres is a marker for longevity. Telomerase is an enzyme that lengthens your telomeres. The changes in the microbiota stimulate the stem cells to increase telomerase.
- ❏ **Yoga/meditation increases glutathione activity.** Glutathione is the principal intracellular antioxidant that protects you from aging. Butyrate, the short-chain fatty acids

produced by gut buddies, influences glutathione levels in the body.

❑ **Yoga/meditation prevents age-related degeneration** by increasing BDNF levels and protecting your neurons from the effects of inflammation. BDNF comes from your gut buddies. Studies have shown that yoga practitioners have significantly greater gray matter concentration in both the prefrontal cortex and the hippocampus and experience fewer cognitive failures. This explains why even though most people lose brain mass as they age, long-term meditators do not.

Online Videos

1. The Gut-Brain Connection (https://youtu.be/oym87kVhqm4)

2. How Neurons Communicate (https://youtu.be/hGDvvUNU-cw)

3. 2-Minute Neuroscience: Glial Cells (https://youtu.be/AwES6R1_9PM)

4. Parkinson's Disease Overview (https://youtu.be/_rP-koFWuoWs)

5. Multiple Sclerosis Overview (https://youtu.be/LaX1hPlJwbc)

6. The Glymphatic System (https://youtu.be/ci5NM-scKJws)

7. Is Olive Oil Healthy? | Dr. Josh Axe (https://youtu.be/dvmb5IM-n5I)

8. Omega-3 Fatty Acid Benefits (https://youtu.be/OM4HjsQleWw)

9. How Meditation Can Reshape Our Brains (https://youtu.be/m8rRzTtP7Tc)

Chapter 7
Look Younger As You Age

Your gut buddies are in charge of your beauty from the inside out. If you've been gaining weight and your skin is getting thinner, more wrinkled, or discolored, you'll see that aging and thinning in the mirror every day. Your gut wall is weakening, allowing more and more unwanted LPSs and bad microbes to enter the bloodstream.

Your Gut Buddies and Your Weight

A study from the University of Chicago Medical Center confirms how your gut microbes are in control of your weight. The researchers found a strain of bacteria living in the upper GI tract that helps you digest and absorb high-fat foods. If you eat a standard Western diet, you will gain more of these bacteria. They'll quickly digest and absorb all the fat you eat. When researchers fed germ-free mice a high-fat diet, they didn't gain any weight because they didn't digest the fat. All the fat came out in their stools. However, when researchers later exposed these germ-free mice to the fat-eating bacteria and fed a high-fat diet, they gained weight because this time the fat-digesting bacteria digested and passed that fat on to them. So it's not the calories you eat that counts; it's the calories "they" make available to you that counts.

Endocrine Disruptors Are Making You Fat

Besides promoting early growth and puberty, these hormone disruptors cause people to gain weight. Estrogen is a hormone that tells the cells of young women to store fat to prepare for an upcoming pregnancy. Endocrine disruptors mimic estrogen in the bodies of both men and women, telling their cells to store fat. As a result, some girls start puberty at eight, and some men have "man boobs" and huge bellies.

Unlike regular hormones that hook up to estrogen receptors, deliver the message and then leave, endocrine disruptors lock into the receptors and never leave, keeping the fat cells switched on to keep storing fat.

Here are some of the most common and harmful endocrine disruptors.

Bisphenol A (BPA)

Since 1957, people have been using the BPA to manufacture plastics, line pipes, and coat the inside of many food and beverage cans. In 2012, the U.S. Food and Drug Administration banned the use of BPA in baby bottles and cans that store baby formula, while Canada and Europe banned it completely. In recent years, scientists have discovered that its "safe" replacement, Bisphenol S (BPS), also has the same endocrine-disrupting properties. To limit your exposure to these products:

- ❏ Avoid canned foods unless you see a label that says "BPA-free lining."
- ❏ Use glassware instead of plasticware to store food.
- ❏ Never heat food in plastic in the microwave. Heat causes BPA to leach out of plastics into food.
- ❏ Use glass or stainless-steel water bottles instead of plastic.
- ❏ Make sure that any plastic toys are BPA-free.

❑ Don't touch cash register receipts because they contain BPA.

Phthalates

Phthalates are industrial chemicals used to soften PVC plastic and as solvents in cosmetics. They are found in wall coverings, vinyl flooring, rubber gloves, plastic wraps, plastic food containers, toys, hair sprays, lubricants, insect repellents, and other household and personal care products.

Phthalates lock onto estrogen receptors in the brain and the thyroid hormone receptors in cells, blocking the real thyroid hormone. This means that people who are producing plenty of thyroid hormones will have symptoms of hypothyroidism, including weight gain. Exposure to phthalates has been linked to DNA damage in sperm, premature birth, and premature breast development in girls.

The major sources of phthalates in humans come from phthalate-laden food packaging. To avoid phthalates:

❑ Avoid most grains, conventionally grown meats, and dairy products.

❑ Use glass or stainless-steel water bottles instead of plastic.

❑ Never heat food in plastic in the microwave.

❑ Read the labels of all personal care products to make sure they say "phthalate-free."

Supplement with Sunscreen

Many sunscreens contain phthalates and other hormone disruptors. When buying sunscreen, look for products with a titanium oxide or zinc oxide base without preservatives. You can also get sunscreen protection by consuming plenty of vitamin C.

Our body uses vitamin C to repair cracks in collagen, the building blocks of connective tissue, skin, and blood vessels. The sun's rays harm your skin by breaking down collagen. Vitamin C can repair it if you have enough of it. If you have insufficient levels of vitamin C, you get wrinkles.

Our body doesn't have the genes to make vitamin C. So we have to consume it. The problem with them is that they are water-soluble, so you excrete vitamin C in your urine. There is also a limit to the amount of vitamin C you can absorb. If you consume more, you're likely to get diarrhea as your body excretes whatever it can't absorb. Since you need plenty of vitamin C to maintain vital, healthy skin and blood vessels, consider a time-released vitamin C supplement.

Arsenic

Arsenic is a poison, an antibiotic that kills your gut buddies, and a hormone disruptor. It will kill you at a dose of 100 milligrams, and smaller doses will make your life shorter and less pleasant instead of strengthening you.

To avoid arsenic:

❏   Stop eating conventionally raised chicken.

❏   Avoid grains, particularly rice, as they contain arsenic.

Azodicarbonamide

Azodicarbonamide is a compound used in the manufacture of synthetic leather products, carpet underlay, and yoga mats. People also use it as a food additive to bleach and increase the shelf life of breads. Most fast-food restaurants use it in their bread products although the European Union and Australia have banned its use in bread. In the United States, Subway has stopped using it in its products.

Studies have shown that azodicarbonamide, when heated or baked, can provoke asthma and allergies, and suppress immune function. This chemical can break down gluten into two of its individual proteins, gliadin and glutenin, making them more available and therefore more irritating to your gut lining.

To avoid azodicarbonamide:

❏ Don't eat fast food.
❏ Avoid grains. If you eat bread, choose organic fermented varieties, such as sourdough.

Blue Light

Blue light inhibits the brain's production of melatonin, the hormone that helps you fall asleep. The resulting sleep deprivation has many adverse health consequences, including obesity. Constant exposure to blue light tricks your body into thinking it's a perpetual summer, stimulating your cells to store fat. Blue light also stimulates the hormones that make you feel hungry (ghrelin) and awake (cortisol), which adds to weight gain.

Televisions, cell phones, computers, electronic devices, and most energy-saving light bulbs emit blue light. To avoid blue light:

❏ Turn off all electronic devices when the sun goes down.
❏ Wear blue-blocker glasses after sunset and before going to bed..
❏ Use red night-lights.
❏ Install an app on your computer to reduce the amount of blue light emitting from your screen. Activate the nighttime lighting mode in the settings on your cell phone, tablet, and computer.

Your Skin Is Your Gut Lining Turned Inside Out

Our skin is our largest barrier to pathogens and our first defense against disease. There are over a trillion microbes living on your skin. We call these bugs your skin flora. Different skin buddies protect your skin in different ways. One species of bacteria secretes antimicrobial substances that help fight pathogenic invaders. Other species use the skin's lipids to generate compounds to ward off microbial threats. Another species secretes lipoteichoic acid (LTA), which prevents the release of inflammatory cytokines so that your skin does not become inflamed. To maximize your skin's protection, it is therefore essential to have a diverse skin bacterial population. Your skin flora should be even more diverse than your gut biome.

However, over the years, we have assumed that having bacteria on our skin was a bad thing. So we started to kill them off with antibacterial cleansers and soaps. As a result, we reduced the diversity of our skin buddies. As we age, the death of our skin buddies and damage to our gut lining are the two predominant causes of skin problems—not sun exposure, genetics, or anything else.

Your skin buddies protect you against sun exposure. There is a strain of bacteria that inhibits the growth of skin cancer. It does this by producing a compound called *6-N-hydroxyaminopurine* (6-HAP), which kills cancer cells but is not toxic to healthy cells. Studies have shown that intravenous injections of 6-HAP reduced the size of skin cancer in mice by half.

An imbalance in the skin flora is a sign of disease. Research has shown that patients with primary immune deficiency conditions have altered skin flora. Their skin flora includes species not found in healthy adults. Patients with eczema have a higher population of bad bugs. When researchers treated these patients with a bacteria normally present in the skin, they saw a significant reduction in symptoms.

Just like your gut buddies, your skin buddies can trigger an immune response to a perceived threat. If your skin buddies overreact, this can lead to chronic inflammation, resulting in skin conditions like eczema.

When your gut microbes are out of balance and allow bad bugs to permeate the gut barrier, bad bugs take over your skin biome, resulting in thinning of skin, age spots, wrinkles, acne, and eczema. That's why patients start to look younger after they begin nourishing their gut buddies, even though they've made no changes to their skincare.

Here are some beneficial ingredients for your skin buddies.

Bonicel (BC30)

BC30 probiotics contain a beneficial spore-forming bacterium that is not digested by stomach acid. Probiotics company Ganeden developed Bonicel from BC30 through a fermentation process. Bonicel contains metabolites from BC30 and is shelf stable for use as cosmetic products. In clinical trials, researchers showed it could decrease coarse skin lines and skin shadows and increase skin hydration, skin smoothness, and skin elasticity.

Polyphenols

Polyphenols are compounds found in fruits, vegetables, grains, tea, coffee, and wine. They give fruits and vegetables their vibrant colors, flavor and aroma. They also have antioxidant properties and anti-aging benefits. Studies have shown that polyphenols stimulate autophagy, boost cognitive performance, and defend your body against free radicals that can enter your body if you're exposed to air pollution, or cigarette smoke. However, most polyphenols are poorly absorbed unless they are first eaten and transformed by the gut microbes.

Olive oil is good for your gut and brain health because it contains high levels of polyphenols. **Resveratrol** is a potent polyphenol found in grapes and red wine. The polyphenols in **pomegranates** help your skin cope with the molecular damage caused by sunlight. Ellagic acid, the polyphenols found in **raspberries** and **blackberries,** help reduce sunspots on the skin when taken orally.

Cranberry seed oil is the best source of polyphenols for your skin. Cranberries are filled with various polyphenols, each of which benefits your skin in its own way:

- ❏ **Catechins** help fight the signs of aging in the skin such as wrinkles and sagging by preventing cell stress and death.
- ❏ **Proanthocyanidins** help protect the skin from the sun's harmful UVA and UVB rays.
- ❏ **Quercetin** helps soothe irritated skin.
- ❏ **Myricetin** hydrates skin cells, keeps skin smooth and firm, prevents skin cell death, and combats damage from sun exposure.

The anti-inflammatory actions of cranberries make them just as good for your gut. You can reap their benefits through the many supplements and cold-pressed oils available on the market.

Polyphenol supplements are widely available, and many skin care brands now include them in their products. Polyphenols are also present in:

- ❏ **Spices**: Cloves, star anise, capers, curry powder, ginger, cumin, cinnamon, and nutmeg.
- ❏ **Dried herbs**: Peppermint, oregano, sage, rosemary, thyme, basil, lemon verbena, and more.
- ❏ **Dark fruits**: Cherries, strawberries, cranberries, raspberries, blueberries, blackberries, huckleberries, and pomegranates.
- ❏ **Natural beverages**: Cocoa, green tea, black tea, and red wine.
- ❏ **Seeds:** Flaxseed (ground only), celery seeds, poppy seeds, black sesame seeds, and Nigella sativa (black cumin or black caraway seed).

- ❏ **Nuts:** Chestnuts, pistachios, and walnuts.
- ❏ **Oils:** Extra-virgin olive oil, sesame oil, and coconut oil.
- ❏ **Dark chocolate** (70 percent cacao or more), and cacao nibs (raw cocoa).

Wild Yam Extract

Wild yams contain multiple compounds that can benefit several parts of the body. They're filled with saponins, compounds in plants that have anti-inflammatory, antimicrobial, and antioxidant properties.

The wild yam is best known for its high quantity of a saponin known as diosgenin. Diosgenin is anti-inflammatory. It enhances DNA synthesis in human skin to restore skin cells. It is also effective as a skin depigmenting agent, helping protect you against nasty age spots. It is used in cosmetics to fight the loss of collagen in the skin, helping you maintain a youthful appearance.

Just like polyphenols, wild yam extract benefits both your skin buddies and your gut buddies with their powerful anti-inflammatory properties. Diosgenin helps stabilize your gastric and intestinal fluids, and helps ease gastrointestinal discomfort stemming from inflammation.

You can buy wild yam supplement as an herb, a capsule, a tablet, or a cream form. You can also buy it as a liquid extract and use it to make tea.

Online Videos

1. Can Your Gut Bacteria Make You Gain Weight? (https://youtu.be/KogCxpXXZ0c)

2. The Great Invasion - Documentary on endocrine disruptors (https://youtu.be/_7RfgJhvyow)

3. How to Reduce Exposure to Bisphenol A (BPA) (https://youtu.be/HAb50e18XHs)

4. Toxins to Avoid: Phthalates (https://youtu.be/APX0-SO0ojFQ)

5. The Best and Worst Vitamin C (https://youtu.be/DnvnKnu7YBI)

6. Azodicarbonamide (ADA) in bread (https://youtu.be/PAk4dmW_6ro)

7. Is Blue Light Bad for You? (https://youtu.be/TX7VFG524ZA)

8. Polyphenols: What They Are, Why They Work, & How to Eat More of Them (https://youtu.be/ZcGCxOt1-Tg)

9. Wild Yam (https://youtu.be/SrZEnpHdx1w)

Part 3

The Longevity Paradox Program

Chapter 8
The Longevity Paradox Foods

In this chapter, we'll cover what foods we eat and what foods to avoid when nourishing your microbiome. A full list of foods appears in the next chapter.

(A) The Best Foods for Gut Buddies

1. Prebiotics

There is a lot of confusion about the difference between probiotics and prebiotics. Probiotics are beneficial gut microbes; prebiotics are the fibrous long-chain sugars they eat. Prebiotics help gut buddies thrive, promote a healthier microbiome in the gut, and crowd out the harmful bacteria. Good sources of prebiotics include yams, jicama, tiger nuts, rutabagas, parsnips, sweet potatoes, mushrooms, taro root (cassava), yucca, celeriac, Jerusalem artichokes (sunchokes), chicory, radicchio, artichokes, and Belgian endive. The last four are also rich in inulin, the favorite food for *Akkermansia muciniphila*, which protect your gut lining.

Here are my favorites:

Ground Flaxseed

Flaxseed has loads of prebiotic fiber, polyphenols, B vitamins, and ALA omega-3 fats. ALA omega-3, which supports the gut lining, is not the same as DHA omega-3 that you need for brain health. Humans cannot convert ALA into DHA. So flaxseeds are great for your gut lining, but you still need fish oil or algae DHA oil for your brain.

You cannot digest flaxseeds in their whole form, so choose ground flaxseeds, flaxseed meal, or flaxseed oil. Once ground, flaxseeds go rancid, so buy them whole and grind them when you use them, or buy the ground meal refrigerated. That goes for the oil: once opened, it will go rancid unless kept cool.

Flaxseeds are also good for your skin buddies. You can use ground flaxseeds to make your own body scrub or use flaxseed oil to moisturize your skin and hair.

Artichokes

Artichokes have loads of prebiotic fiber, vitamins (A, B, C, and E), and minerals (calcium, potassium, and magnesium). They also have lots of antioxidants and polyphenols, which help your liver.

Leeks

Leeks have tons of polyphenols and allicin, a compound that increases your blood vessels' flexibility and reduces cholesterol. Use them in salads and soups.

Okra

Okra is a great source of prebiotic fiber, vitamins C and A, iron, phosphorus, and zinc. Half of its carbohydrates are prebiotic fiber. The mucus in okra binds to lectins!

Jicama

Jicama is high in the prebiotic fiber inulin and vitamin C. A 100-gram serving of jicama supplies 40 percent of your daily vitamin C needs.

Cruciferous Veggies

Cruciferous vegetables are those in the broccoli and cabbage family. They contain tons of fiber, vitamins, minerals, antioxidants, and compounds that strengthen both the gut barrier and the immune system.

The Chicory Family

Chicories are like lettuces, but heartier and with a bitter edge. The chicory family includes escarole, curly endive, radicchio, and Belgian endive. They have tons of prebiotic fiber inulin that feeds the bacterium *Akkermansia* that strengthens the gut lining.

Nuts

Some "nuts" are not nuts. For example, cashews are seeds full of lectins. Other "nuts" such as peanuts are legumes loaded with lectins. Real nuts feed the butyrate-producing microbes in the gut. As a result, they support heart health, regulate blood pressure levels, and protect against gallstones, diabetes, and inflammation. The best choices are walnuts, macadamia nuts, hazelnuts, and pistachios. You should eat a handful of nuts every day.

Mushrooms

Mushrooms are the highest dietary source of two important anti-aging compounds—ergothioneine and glutathione. These two antioxidants protect you from free radicals and help you stay young. They have large amounts of polysaccharides, which feed your gut buddies and enhance your immune system. Unlike some foods that lose their nutritional value after cooking, cooking doesn't affect the key polyphenols in mushrooms. Mushrooms also have loads of spermidine, a longevity-promoting compound found in high levels among centenarians. Studies have shown that spermidine increases life span and is cardioprotective.

2. Low-Sugar Fruits

Because of their low-sugar content, you can eat them in large quantities year-round.

Avocados

Avocados have loads of prebiotic fibers, vitamins C and E, potassium, folate, and the same healthy monounsaturated fat found in olive oil, which supports brain functions. Your skin buddies also like avocados. Try mashing a ripe avocado and using it as a DIY skin mask or a deep conditioner for your hair. The fatty acids in avocados can help your skin's natural oil barrier stay strong, protecting you from the aging effects of sun damage.

Green Bananas

A ripe banana is rich in potassium and sugar. Green bananas have lower fructose content and lots of resistant starch, which your gut buddies love. Like avocados, these low-sugar fruits nourish your hair and skin. Try mashing half an avocado and half a green banana together and using the mixture as a hair and/or skin mask.

Raspberries, Blackberries, and Mulberries

These berries have loads of prebiotic fiber, polyphenols, and vitamins A, C, and K.

Figs and Coconuts

Figs are flowers, not fruits, and coconuts are tree nuts! Most of the sugar in figs come from prebiotic fiber. You can bake with coconut flour or sprinkle shredded coconut on top of grilled veggies. Just make sure you're using unsweetened figs and coconuts.

3. Healthy Fats

Your choice of fat is important because they are either inflammatory or anti-inflammatory. Omega-3 (DHA and EPA) of fish oil are anti-inflammatory, but you need a bit of salicylic acid—the active ingredient in aspirin—to get the anti-inflammatory effects. I recommend taking an 81-milligram enteric-coated aspirin a few times a week to activate the fish oil you've been consuming.

We know that omega-6 fats are inflammatory. However, a large study found that men with the highest levels of omega-6 fat AA and omega-6 fat linoleic acid (LA) had the lowest risk of cardiovascular deaths. Another study showed that athletes who supplemented with AA improved their performance and reduced the level of interleukin (IL-16), a marker for inflammation. Half of your brain's fat is omega-3 fat DHA, while the other half is omega-6 fat arachidonic acid (AA). These fats are there to prevent inflammation in your brain.

Omega-3s EPA and DHA are important for your brain health. Studies have shown that people with high levels of EPA and DHA in their blood have the largest brain size and memory areas. Some vegans don't know that short-chain omega-3 fats in flaxseed oil don't convert to EPA or DHA. They should supplement with algae-derived DHA. Omega-3 supplements have also reduced disruptive behavior in healthy children. A study at Oxford University showed that students supplemented with algae-derived DHA exhibited improved learning and behavior. Students afflicted with ADHD saw an improvement in their symptoms.

Shellfish are the best choice for both long-chain omega-3 and omega-6 AA fats. Egg yolk contains loads of omega-6 AA. Here are other interesting fats and oils.

Perilla Seed Oil

Perilla seed oil is oil from the perilla plant, which is in the same family as mint and basil. It supports both your joint and heart health. Like flaxseeds, they contain omega-3 ALA fats, which benefit your cardiovascular system. It also contains rosmarinic acid, which has antibacterial, antiviral, antioxidant, and anti-inflammatory properties. Perilla oil works great as the fat in stir-fries, eggs, and salads.

MCT Oil

MCT stands for "medium-chain triglycerides." Your liver can convert MCT oil into ketones, which your mitochondria use as fuel when your sugar supplies run low.

Olive Oil

Olive oil has tons of polyphenols and therefore is a miracle drug for longevity.

Other good fats

Macadamia nut oil
Walnut oil
Avocado oil
Thrive algae oil
Citrus-flavored cod-liver oil
Coconut oil.

4. Dairy Alternatives

Most conventional dairy products are inflammatory because they contain the casein A1 protein that stimulates inflammation. Here are some options for your gut buddies.

Goat Cheese/Yogurt/Butter

Milk from a cow, goat, lamb, or water buffalo contains large amounts of insulin-like growth factor 1 (IGF-1), which promotes not only growth but also cancer and aging. Moreover, they all contain milk sugars such as lactose.

Goat and sheep cheese lack IGF-1 and sugars because IGF-1 is water-soluble and sugars got used up in fermentation. They are the best options for animal protein. Your best yogurt choice is coconut yogurt which lacks animal protein and IGF-1..

Coconut Milk and Yogurt

You make coconut milk by blending and straining the meat of the coconut. Coconut milk has lots of lauric acid, a saturated fat. Use only unsweetened coconut milk or yogurt. If you see sugar on the label of unsweetened coconut yogurt, don't worry. Coconut meat has no sugar. People add sugar to make coconut yogurt because the bacteria that make yogurt have to have sugar to ferment.

Ghee

When butter melts, it separates into liquid fat and milk solids. The milk solids comprise the casein protein and lactose. People make ghee by removing the milk solids from melted butter. So it's safe to eat ghee even from casein A1 cows. Ghee is a staple of South Asian and Indian cuisines. You can store without refrigeration because it won't go rancid.

5. Millet Is Not Just for the Birds

Most grains are inflammatory and aging because of their high levels of lectins. However, millet, a key seed in birdseed, is an exception. Millet is lectin-free, and it is also high in fiber and rich in magnesium and potassium. It is the best gluten-free option for people suffering from celiac disease.

6. Coffee Fruit

Studies have shown that coffee consumption reduces the risk of death. If you don't drink coffee, you can eat the fruit of the coffee beans. Coffee fruit has tons of antioxidants and polyphenols that help boost your immune system, protect your body against free-radical damage, and fight inflammation. It also has loads of flavonoids, plant chemicals that help keep your blood vessels flexible and young. Coffee fruit also supports cognitive function by boosting brain-derived neurotrophic factor (BDNF), which helps your brain grow new neurons. Raw coffee fruit is hard to find unless you live on a coffee farm. However, the dried form is easy to find in supplements.

7. Extra-Dark Chocolate

The real benefit of chocolate lies in plant-derived cacao. Flavonoids in cacao can boost your brain health and increase blood flow to the cerebral cortex, the brain structure most affected by aging. In one study, people who ate small amounts of dark chocolate for three months had a better memory, processing speed, and attentiveness. Other research has shown a notable improvement in memory retention and new learning in elderly adults after consuming dark chocolates.

Look for chocolate that contains at least 72 percent cacao. The darker the chocolate, the better. Milk chocolate is mostly sugar and has no health benefits. Avoid dutched or alkali chocolate products; the dutching process destroys the health-promoting polyphenols in chocolate.

8. Green Tea

Green tea improves symptoms and reduces the pathology of autoimmune diseases by suppressing autoimmune T cells and their inflammatory cytokines. I recommend you drink about five cups of green and mint teas a day to keep inflammation at bay even if you don't have an autoimmune condition.

For extra longevity, try organic *pu-erh* tea. Studies have shown that pu-erh tea reduces the oxidation of lipids and lowers the levels of iron, which promotes aging. Pu-erh tea also promotes the growth of *Akkermansia muciniphila*, which protects the gut lining.

(B) Avoid These Gut-Destroying Foods

1. Simple Sugars and Starches

Simple sugar—glucose, fructose, and sucrose—is the food of choice for bad bugs and cancer cells. In the past, fruits were only available during the summer and fall. But now fruit, sweet treats, and real or fake sugars are available around the clock. This is a driving factor of the obesity epidemic.

Besides table sugar, sweets, and other obvious forms of sugar, avoid the following fruits that are highest in sugar.

Grapes

Grapes are tiny sugar bombs. However, when fermented into wine or vinegar, grapes are good for you. They're a high-polyphenol food, and the fermentation process removes the sugar, making them much safer. So enjoy plenty of balsamic vinegar and moderate amounts of red wine. If you don't already drink alcohol, don't start!

Mangoes

Mangoes are full of sugars: glucose, fructose, and sucrose. Unripe mangoes are pure oligosaccharides. As a mango ripens, all three types of sugar increase. Bad bugs love ripe mangoes while your gut buddies love unripe mangoes. You can enjoy unripe mangoes in salads.

Ripe Bananas

80 percent of green bananas are resistant starch. But once it ripens, this starch gets converted to sugar. So stay away from ripe bananas and opt for unripe green bananas.

Lychees

Lychees are chock-full of sugar—about 7 teaspoons per cup. You should avoid them.

Apples

One medium apple contains 5 teaspoons of sugar. Apples are also high in soluble fiber, so they're not a complete no-go. But stick to in-season (August–November) apples, and think of them as a special treat, not a daily snack.

Pineapple

One cup of pineapple contains 4 teaspoons of sugar. You should avoid them.

Pears

A medium-ripe pear contains about 17 grams of sugar. However, crispy pears such as Anjou and an unripe Bartlett are full of resistant starches. Eat them just before they ripen.

2. Sugar Substitutes

Sugar substitutes such as sucralose, saccharin, and aspartame are just as bad as actual sugar, if not worse. They alter the gut microbiome by encouraging bad bugs to take over. A recent study showed that consuming sucralose (Splenda) promoted higher blood glucose and insulin levels in humans. Sucralose converts into toxic compounds that may persist in your body.

Artificial sweeteners also promote weight gain. They send the same pleasure signal to your brain as sugars do. When the calories don't make it to your bloodstream, your brain tells your body to go back and get more sugar.

3. Conventional Dairy Products

Most American dairy products have casein A1 protein, which can spark autoimmune attacks. Most people who complain of lactose intolerance are struggling with casein A1 intolerance. Casein A2 is present in the milk of goats, sheep, and water buffalo and in imported cheeses from France, Italy, and Switzerland. You can enjoy these products without destroying your health.

4. Bad Fats

Saturated Fats

Recall that bacteria produce LPS molecules as they divide and die in your gut. The LPSs travel through your gut wall by riding on saturated fats and cause inflammation.

Peanut Oil

Peanut oil is full of lectins, which leads to an autoimmune attack on the arteries. Studies have shown that peanut oil consumption leads to atherosclerosis and coronary narrowing.

Other fats to avoid

Grape seed oil
Corn oil
Cottonseed oil
Safflower oil
Sunflower oil
Partially hydrogenated vegetable or canola oil

Online Videos

1. Modulating the Gut Microbiome – the Role of Probiotics and Prebiotics (https://youtu.be/ZnRwbDWz2ek)

2. Prebiotic vs. Probiotic: What's the Difference? (https://youtu.be/kpzVCmtAqqQ)

3. Prebiotics Foods | Prebiotics are good for Digestive Health (https://youtu.be/G0KuzJRjGVU)

4. Top 10 Fruits Low In Sugar (https://youtu.be/6zcA--FRiBQ)

5. The Fats You Should Eat to Help You Eat Less (https://youtu.be/xJY0DMTV_q4)

6. MCT Oil 101 (https://youtu.be/dZVfHfYYi7w)

7. 5 Incredible Health Benefits Of Millet (https://youtu.be/PFeAvnIRF-c)

8. What is Coffee Fruit? (https://youtu.be/2RClRCt-t0Wo)

9. Is Eating Dark Chocolate Actually Healthy? (https://youtu.be/OAhemM7yBHg)

Chapter 9
The Longevity Paradox Meal Plan

In the 1950s, Luigi Cornaro published one of the best books on longevity. When he was 40, he was in poor health, a condition attributed to excessive eating and drinking. On the advice of his doctor, he adhered to a calorie restriction diet, which he maintained well into his old age. He began writing his book *Discorsi della Vita Sobria: Discourses On the Temperate Life* when he was in his eighties. The book, which described his regimen, was extremely successful. He added a new chapter as he reached each five- or ten-year milestone thereafter. He remained in vigorous health until he died a young man at 102.

It's no coincidence that Luigi Cornaro reached this robust state of health after restricting his calorie intake. On the *Longevity Paradox* program, you, too, will plan periods of calorie restriction, but you'll do it without suffering. Each month, you will break down your days as follows:

- ❏ **Fast-Mimicking Days.** Five consecutive days a month, you will eliminate animal protein and limit calories to 900 a day.
- ❏ **Free Days.** On most days, you will eat as much as you like of the Longevity Paradox foods.

❏ **Brain-Wash Days.** Once or twice a week, you will skip dinner or eat it very early to make sure your blood can flow to your brain as soon as you fall asleep.

❏ **Optional Calorie Restriction Days.** If you choose, you will consume only 600 calories a day once or twice a week to get extra longevity benefits.

❏ **Optional Intensive Care Cleanse.** This program, which includes more fasting and brain-wash days, will give your mitochondrial function an extra boost.

Let's break down each of these components and look at how and what you'll be eating all month long.

Fast-Mimicking Days

Research by Dr. Valter Longo at the University of Southern California has shown that a monthly five-day modified vegan fast gives you the same longevity-boosting results as a month of a traditional calorie-restricted diet does. So you can restrict calories for only five consecutive days out of the month and still reap the benefits of an entire month of calorie restriction.

Begin the program by doing five fast-mimicking days in a row. It will allow you to change the makeup of your gut microbes. Once your gut buddies are in good shape, they will make it much easier for you to follow the rest of the program.

In these five days, you will eliminate animal protein and limit calories to 900 a day. If you get hungry and need something more, have a tablespoon of MCT oil up to three times a day.

This is what you'll be eating during these five days, starting with what not to eat.

(A) Foods to Avoid

- ❏ All dairy products
- ❏ All grains and pseudograins
- ❏ All fruits, including all seeded vegetables
- ❏ Sugars of all kinds.
- ❏ Unapproved seeds
- ❏ Eggs and dairy products.
- ❏ Soy products
- ❏ Nightshade plants (eggplant, peppers, tomatoes, potatoes)
- ❏ Corn, soy, canola, and other vegetable oils
- ❏ Meat, chicken, and all other animal products
- ❏ All other foods on the "Gut-Destroying Bad Bug Favorites" list

(B) Foods to Include

Vegetables

All vegetables should be organic, fresh or frozen. If fresh, they should be in season.

- ❏ **Cruciferous veggies:** Bok choy, broccoli, Brussels sprouts, Swiss chard, any color and type of cabbage, cauliflower, kale, mustard greens, collard greens, rapini, kohlrabi, watercress, mizuna, and arugula.
- ❏ **Greens:** Belgian endive, lettuce, spinach, dandelion greens, and chicory.
- ❏ **Other veggies:** Treviso, radicchio, artichokes and asparagus. celery and fennel.
- ❏ **Root veggies:** Radishes, yams, taro root, jicama, yucca, cassava, turnips, rutabagas, and horseradish.
- ❏ **Fresh herbs:** Mint, parsley, sage, basil, cilantro, garlic, onions, leeks, and chives.

❏ **Ocean vegetables**: Kelp, seaweed, and nori.

Protein

You go vegan for these five days. That means no eggs, meat, chicken, or dairy products. Acceptable sources of plant-based protein for these five days include:

❏ Tempeh (fermented soy, without grains).
❏ Hemp tofu and hemp seeds.
❏ Pressure-cooked legumes such as lentils and beans.
❏ Hilary's Millet Cakes.
❏ Approved nuts and seeds.

Fats and Oils

Acceptable vegetable fat sources for these five days include:

❏ **Avocado**—You can have a whole one each day.
❏ **Olives** of any kind.
❏ **Nuts**: Walnuts, macadamia nuts, pistachios, hazelnuts, pine nuts, Marcona almonds, and blanched almond flour.
❏ **Oils**: First-cold-pressed olive oil, avocado oil, coconut oil, macadamia nut oil, MCT oil, perilla oil, sesame seed oil, walnut oil, hemp seed oil, and flaxseed oil.

Condiments and Seasonings

Avoid all commercially prepared salad dressings and sauces. Use:

❏ Fresh lemon juice.
❏ Vinegars.
❏ Mustard.
❏ Freshly ground black pepper.
❏ Iodized sea salt.
❏ All herbs and spices except red chili pepper flakes.

Beverages

Avoid all sodas (including diet sodas), sports drinks, lemonade, and other commercially prepared beverages. Enjoy at least eight cups of tap or filtered water a day, and:

- ❏ Mineral water.
- ❏ Tea—green, black, or herbal.
- ❏ Coffee (black or with unsweetened almond, hemp, or coconut milk).
- ❏ You can sweeten your coffee or tea with stevia extract (Sweet-Leaf), Just Like Sugar (inulin), or monk fruit.

(C) Meal Plan

Day 1

Breakfast Green Smoothie
Snack Romaine Lettuce Boats Filled with Guacamole
Lunch Arugula Salad with Hemp Tofu, Grain-Free Tempeh, or Cauliflower "Steak" and Lemon Vinaigrette
Snack Romaine Lettuce Boats Filled with Guacamole
Dinner Cabbage-Kale Sauté with Grain-Free Tempeh and Avocado

Day 2

Breakfast Green Smoothie
Snack Romaine Lettuce Boats Filled with Guacamole
Lunch Romaine Salad with Avocado, Cilantro Pesto, and Grain-Free Tempeh
Snack Romaine Lettuce Boats Filled with Guacamole
Dinner Lemony Brussels Sprouts, Kale, and Onions with Cabbage "Steak"

Day 3

Breakfast Green Smoothie

Snack Romaine Lettuce Boats Filled with Guacamole

Lunch Hemp Tofu-Arugula-Avocado Seaweed Wrap with Cilantro Dipping Sauce

Snack Romaine Lettuce Boats Filled with Guacamole

Dinner Roasted Broccoli with Cauliflower "Rice" and Sautéed Onions

Day 4

Breakfast Green Smoothie

Snack Romaine Lettuce Boats Filled with Guacamole

Lunch Longevity Leek Soup

Snack Romaine Lettuce Boats Filled with Guacamole

Dinner Hemp Tofu-Arugula-Avocado Seaweed Wrap with Cilantro Dipping Sauce

Day 5

Breakfast Green Smoothie

Snack Romaine Lettuce Boats Filled with Guacamole

Lunch Creamy Cauliflower Parmesan Soup

Snack Romaine Lettuce Boats Filled with Guacamole

Dinner Cauliflower "Fried Rice"

Free Days

After you finish your five-day "fast," you can begin the free day portion of the plan by eating as much as you like of the Longevity Paradox food. However, be mindful of your protein intake. You'll get plenty of protein from veggies, nuts, mushrooms, and pressure-cooked lentils and by recycling the mucus in your gut. You can meet your protein needs for an entire day with a scoop of whey protein powder, two eggs, one protein bar, or three ounces of chicken or wild fish. Other than that, enjoy these foods.

(A) Longevity-Promoting Acceptable Foods

Oils

Olive oil	Walnut oil
Algae oil	Red palm oil
Coconut oil	Rice bran oil
Macadamia oil	Sesame oil
MCT oil	Flavored cod-liver oil
Avocado oil	Perilla oil

Sweeteners

Stevia (SweetLeaf)	Luo han guo (aka monk fruit)
Just Like Sugar (inulin)	Erythritol (Swerve)
Inulin	Xylitol
Yacon	Monk fruit

Nuts and Seeds (1/2 cup per day)

Macadamia nuts	Hazelnuts
Pili nuts	Chestnuts
Baruka nuts	Brazil nuts (in limited amounts)
Walnuts	Pine nuts
Pistachios	Flaxseeds
Pecans	Hemp seeds
Coconut meat, milk or cream (unsweetened)	Hemp protein powder
	Psyllium seeds or powder

Olives

All

Coconut Yogurt (plain)

Dark Chocolate

72% cacao or greater (1 ounce per day)

Vinegars

All

Herbs and Seasonings

❑   All except chili pepper flakes

❑   Miso

Bars

Adapt Bar: coconut and chocolate

10. Flours

Coconut

Almond

Hazelnut

Sesame (and seeds)

Chestnut

Cassava

Green banana

Sweet potato

Tiger nut

Grape seed

Arrowroot

Ice Cream

Coconut milk dairy-free frozen dessert (the So Delicious blue label, which contains only 1 gram of sugar per serving)

"Foodles" (my name for acceptable noodles)

Cappello's gluten-free fettuccine and other pastas

Pasta Slim shirataki noodles

Kelp noodles

Miracle Noodle brand pasta

Miracle Rice

Korean sweet potato noodles

Palmini Hearts of Palm Linguine

Wine (6 ounces per day)

Red

Spirits (1 ounce per day)

Dark spirits like bourbon, scotch, dark tequila, dark rum, cognac, and gin. Avoid vodka.

Fruits (limit all to their seasons except avocado)

Avocados

Blueberries

Raspberries

Blackberries

Strawberries

Cherries

Crispy pears

Pomegranates

Dates

Kiwis

Apples

Citrus fruits (no juices)

Nectarines

Peaches

Plums

Apricots

Figs

Vegetables

Cruciferous Vegetables

Broccoli

Brussels sprouts

Cauliflower

Bok choy

Jerusalem artichokes (sunchokes)

Hearts of palm

Cilantro

Parsley

Napa cabbage

Chinese cabbage

Swiss chard

Arugula

Watercress

Collards

Kohlrabi

Kale

Green and red cabbage

Raw sauerkraut

Kimchi

Other Vegetables

Treviso, radicchio

Chicory

Curly endive

Nopales cactus leaves

Celery

Onions

Leeks

Chives

Scallions

Carrots (raw)

Carrot greens

Artichokes

Beets (raw)

Okra

Asparagus

Garlic

Mushrooms

Leafy Greens

Romaine

Red- and green-leaf lettuce

Mesclun (baby greens)

Spinach

Endive

Dandelion greens

Butter lettuce

Fennel

Escarole

Mustard greens

Mizuna

Parsley

Basil

Mint

Purslane

Perilla

Algae

Seaweed

Sea vegetables

Daikon radish

Radishes

Resistant Starches

- ❏ Tortillas (Siete brand—only those made with cassava and co-conut flour or almond flour)
- ❏ Bread and bagels made by Barely Bread

- ❏ Julian Bakery Paleo Wraps (made with coconut flour)
- ❏ The Real Coconut Café Tortillas and Chips

In Moderation

Green plantains

Green bananas

Baobab fruit

Cassava (tapioca)

Sweet potatoes or yams

Blue or purple sweet potatoes

Rutabaga

Parsnips

Yucca

Celery root (celeriac)

Glucomannan (konjac root)

Persimmon

Jicama

Taro root

Turnips

Tiger nuts

Green mango

Millet

Sorghum "popcorn"

Green papaya

Plant-Based Protein

- ❏ **Quorn**: Chik'n Tenders, Grounds, Chik'n Cutlets, Turk'y Roast, Bacon-Style Slices
- ❏ Hemp tofu
- ❏ Hilary's Root Veggie Burger
- ❏ Tempeh (grain free only)

Pressure-Cooked Legumes (or Eden brand canned)

Lentils (preferred)

Black soybeans

Chickpeas

Adzuki beans

Other beans

Peas

(B) Disease-Promoting, Life-Shortening Foods to Avoid

Refined, Starchy Foods

Pasta

Potatoes

Potato chips

Milk

Bread

Tortillas

Pastry

Wheat, rye, barley, rice, quinoa, soy, corn flours

Crackers

Cookies

Cereal

Sugar

Agave

Sweet One or Sunett (acesulfame-K)

Splenda (sucralose)

NutraSweet (aspartame)

Sweet'N Low (saccharin)

Diet drinks

Maltodextrin

Vegetables

Peas

Sugar snap peas

Legumes

Green beans

Chickpeas (including as hummus)

Soy products

Tofu

Edamame

Soy protein

Textured vegetable protein

Pea protein

All beans, including sprouts

All lentils

Nuts and Seeds

Pumpkin seeds

Sunflower seeds

Chia seeds

Peanuts

Cashews

Fruits (some are incorrectly called vegetables)

Cucumbers	Eggplant
Zucchini	Tomatoes
Pumpkins	Bell peppers
Squash (any kind)	Chili peppers
Melon (any kind)	Goji berries

Non–Southern European Cow Milk Products (these contain casein A1)

Yogurt (including Greek yogurt), ice cream, and frozen yogurt.

Cheese

Ricotta, cottage cheese, and kefir.

Grains, Sprouted Grains, Pseudograins, and Grasses

Wheat	Barley
Einkorn wheat	Buckwheat
Farro	Kashi
Kamut	Spelt
Oats	Corn
Quinoa	Corn products
Rye	Corn syrup
Bulgur	Popcorn
White rice	Wheatgrass
Brown rice	Barley grass
Wild rice	

Oils

Soy	Safflower
Grape seed	Sunflower
Corn	"Vegetable"
Peanut	Canola
Cottonseed	

(C) Acceptable Animal Protein Sources in Limited Amounts

Dairy Products (1 ounce cheese or 4 ounces yogurt per day)

- ❏ Real Parmesan (Parmigiano-Reggiano), French or Italian butter, Buffalo butter (available at Trader Joe's), and ghee.
- ❏ **Goat** yogurt (plain), milk, cheese, kefir, and butter
- ❏ **Sheep** cheese, yogurt (plain), and kefir.
- ❏ Aged French, Italian, or Swiss cheese, and buffalo mozzarella
- ❏ **Casein A2 milk** (as creamer only)
- ❏ Organic heavy cream, sour cream, and cream cheese

Fish (wild caught; 4 ounces per day maximum)

- ❏ Whitefish, including cod, sea bass, redfish, red or pink snapper.
- ❏ Freshwater bass, perch, and pike.
- ❏ Alaskan halibut and salmon
- ❏ Tuna, sardines, anchovies, and smelt.
- ❏ Hawaiian fish, like mahi-mahi, opakapaka, ono.

Shellfish (wild caught):

Shrimp, crab, lobster, scallops, calamari (squid), clams, oysters, mussels (farmed okay), abalone (farmed okay), and sea urchin (uni).

Pastured Poultry (not free range; 4 ounces per day)

Chicken, turkey, goose, duck, pheasant, quail, and ostrich.

Eggs:

Pastured, non-soy or -corn fed, or omega-3 eggs (up to 4 daily), but limit whites, e.g., make an omelet with 4 yolks and 1 white)

Meat (grass fed and finished; 4 ounces per day maximum; once per week maximum).

Bison, venison, boar, elk, pork, lamb, beef, prosciutto, bresaola, liver, and other organ meats

(D) Meal Plans

Day 1

Breakfast Blueberry Miso Muffins

Lunch Creamy Cauliflower Parmesan Soup with a side of Bitter Green Salad with Walnut Blue Cheese Dressing

Dinner Roasted Broccoli with Miso Walnut Sauce, Mushroom and Thyme Braised Tempeh over cauliflower rice

Snacks & Dessert 1/2 avocado with Miso Sesame Dressing; piece of in-season fruit

Day 2

Breakfast Toasted Millet "Grits" with Spicy Eggs

Lunch Roasted Broccoli with Miso Walnut Sauce, Mushroom and Thyme Braised Tempeh over cauliflower rice

Dinner Lentil Broccoli Curry with Ginger Coconut Cauliflower "Rice"

Snacks & Dessert Basil Lentil "Pâté"; Mexican Chocolate "Rice" Pudding

Day 3

Breakfast Blueberry Miso Muffins (leftover from day 1)

Lunch Lentil Broccoli Curry with Ginger Coconut Cauliflower "Rice"

Dinner Spinach Salad with Lentil-Cauliflower Fritters

Snacks & Dessert 1/2 avocado with Miso Sesame Dressing; Mexican Chocolate "Rice" Pudding

Brain-Wash Days

Recall that your body needs at least four hours to finish digesting your last meal before you go to sleep for your glymphatic system to wash out your brain at night. This is how you can avoid the toxic buildup of amyloid in the brain that can lead to degenerative disease. I recommend that you skip dinner once a week if you are in good health, more often if you suffer from a degenerative disease. On a brain-wash day, you will stop eating after lunch. You can condense all three meals into the first half of the day if you wish, eating your last meal no later than 4:00 p.m.

This will also allow you to take advantage of the benefits of intermittent fasting. For the best results, make sure that eighteen hours pass before your next meal. Limiting your eating to a six-hour window daily stimulates autophagy, your cells' recycling program. So by just skipping dinner and delaying your breakfast, you get a cleaned-out brain, younger cells, and a renewed gut barrier.

Optional Calorie Restriction Days

If you want to go all in on calorie restriction, try the 5:2 diet. Here, you reduce your daily calories to 600 calories per day on two days of your choice each week. The other five days of the week are free days. I advise doing your calorie restrictions on Monday and Thursday. You can change these days each week to accommodate your schedule.

There are 600 calories in three Quest bars, or seven to eight hard-boiled eggs. Salads work well on these days, but remember that one teaspoon of olive oil has 120 calories. I recommend eating lots of raw and cooked veggies with a bit of olive oil and a small amount of a concentrated vegetable or nut protein on these days to get maximum nutrition while enjoying calorie restriction.

Optional Intensive Care Cleanse

Recall that cancer cells and certain immune cells cannot use fat as fuel. They must go through an inefficient sugar fermentation process to derive energy. If you have cancer or are suffering from an autoimmune disease, Parkinson's disease, or dementia, the intensive care cleanse provides your mitochondria with the fuel they need while starving the cells that cause your condition.

For this program, you'll follow the list of your gut buddies' favorite foods here that you will eat on free days with the following changes.

❏ Eliminate all fruits and seeded vegetables—their fructose feeds the cancer cells—except for avocados, green bananas and plantains, green mangoes, and green papayas.

❏ Continue to use olive oil as your main source of fat, but opt for MCT oil, coconut oil, or ghee as other fat sources. Eat as much of these fats as you can.

❏ Eat macadamias as your preferred nuts, with smaller amounts of other nuts.

❏ You can still treat yourself to extra-dark chocolate, but be sure it contains at least 90% cacao. Lindt makes a good 90% cacao chocolate bar. Trader Joe's carries a 100% cacao bar with cacao nibs.

❏ Eat only 2 ounces of animal proteins—the size of a quarter of a deck of cards—a day, in the form of wild fish, shellfish, and mollusks. If you have cancer, avoid all animal protein.

❏ Egg yolks have one of two fats your brain needs to function.. Try a four-yolk, one-whole-egg omelet cooked in coconut oil or ghee and filled with sliced avocado, mushrooms, and onions and sprinkled with turmeric and black pepper.

❏ Avocados, hemp seeds, coconut oils, are a good source of fat and plant protein. Walnuts have the highest plant protein content of the nut choices.

Putting it all together, let's look at what one month on the Longevity Paradox program looks like.

Week 1

❏ 5 fast-mimicking days followed by 2 free days

Weeks 2, 3, and 4

❏ 4 free days, 2 calorie restriction days of your choice, and 1 brain-wash day; or

❏ 6 free days and 1 brain-wash day; or

❏ 5 free days and 2 brain-wash days; or

❏ add as many days as you wish of the optional intensive care cleanse.

You can customize the program to suit your needs. However, if you are already suffering from dementia, type 2 diabetes, an autoimmune condition, or other diseases of aging caused by dysbiosis, you may need to follow the protocol to the letter.

Online Videos

1. The Secret To A Longer Life? Stop Eating! (https:// youtu.be/oB_Ea_fkA68)

2. Longevity & Why I now eat One Meal a Day (https:// youtu.be/PKfR6bAXr-c)

3. 5 2 Diets (https://youtu.be/VWtaLLjJzn4)

4. How To Optimize Your Diet For Longevity with Dr. Steven Gundry (https://youtu.be/hoyLBCi-KxA)

Chapter 10
The Longevity Paradox
Lifestyle Plan

This pillar of the *Longevity Paradox* program involves stressing your cells through your lifestyle choices. The first part of the program focuses on habits that will stress and strengthen your cells. The second part focuses on the habits that will allow them to recover. Alternating between periods of stress and rest will benefit your gut buddies and help you achieve a long health span.

Part 1: Conquer Stress

Start off by completing this exercise twice a day. It will give you an instant burst of energy while strengthening all the muscles in your body.

Step 1: The Longevity Paradox Exercise Plan

First Minute: Jog in Place

Move your legs and arms as though you're running while staying in place. If this is too much for you, you can do it while sitting upright in a chair.

Second Minute: Classic Crunches

Lie on your back with your knees bent, arms pointed toward your feet. Focus on lifting your head and shoulders up using your abs, not your neck or your arms. You don't need to sit all the way up. Repeat as many times as you can for one minute. If this is too much strain on your neck, you can support your head with your hands, but don't pull up with them.

Third Minute: Plank

To do a plank, get to the top of a "push-up" position and hold it for one minute. If this is easy for you, do push-ups for that minute instead. If it is too hard, perform the plank resting on your elbows with your forearms out front.

Fourth Minute: Squats

Stand with your feet a little wider than hip-width apart. Inhale and slowly bend your knees while keeping your chest forward and your head lifted. Bend as deeply as you can, then return to a standing position. Do as many repetitions as you can in one minute. If you feel unbalanced, hold on to a counter or the back of a chair with one hand.

Fifth Minute: Meditation

Start by either sitting up straight or lying on your back. Focus on inhaling deeply through your nose and exhaling completely through your mouth. With each exhalation, think about relaxing your muscles, starting with your feet, then your knees and thighs, and so on.

A Prescription to Play!

Get outside as much as you can and get moving. If possible, take your daily walks up and down hills to stress more muscles and reap even greater benefits.

Another simple exercise is to bounce on a mini-trampoline. Many rebounders come with a pole or a handle for balance. To get started, stand on your mini-trampoline with your feet shoulder-width apart. Bend your knees and lightly bounce up and down. Do this for one minute. Rest for one minute.

HIIT for Fun

High-intensity interval training (HIIT) burns more fat than traditional exercise does. While traditional aerobic exercise can weaken the immune system, HIIT doesn't have that effect. In addition to doing your five-minute daily routines, do a ten-minute HIIT routine three times a week. You can choose any form of exercise you prefer: walking, running, cycling, spinning, or jumping jacks. Work as hard as you can for thirty seconds or so, followed by an equal amount of recovery time. As you get stronger, you might extend your bursts of intensity to a minute. Just be sure to give yourself adequate recovery afterward. Continue until your ten minutes are up.

Step 2: Cook Your Cells—Just a Little

When temporarily stressed by extreme temperatures, your cells produce *heat-shock proteins* that protect you against all kinds of threats. Once a week, try to spend some time in a sauna or take a nice hot bath. Recent studies have shown that a hot bath relieves mild depression better than antidepressants. To avoid overstressing your cells, start your bath with warm water, and then keep letting out some water and adding more hot water.

Step 3: Toughen Up for the Winter

Exposure to cold temperatures has a similar effect as heat exposure. It also stimulates your gut buddies to produce more of two beneficial neurotransmitters, *GABA* and *serotonin*, both of which help extend life span.

To take advantage of these benefits, you can take a daily "Scottish shower." To do so, start your shower with warm water as usual and then gradually cool the water down until you are running nothing but cold water. You can also buy a cold vest—a vest with removable cold packs—and wear it for a few hours a day.

Your skin buddies also love a Scottish shower. Hot water strips out the nourishing oils they produce for your skin and hair. Cold water leaves these important oils intact.

Part 2: Rejuvenate

Step 1: Prioritize Sleep

Your body needs adequate sleep every night. During deep sleep, the glymphatic system "washes" your brain so it doesn't build up amyloid that leads to Alzheimer's and other neurodegenerative diseases. This program recommends you to skip dinner once a week so your blood can flow to your brain to complete that important cleanse when you get to sleep.

Lack of sleep may lead to weight gain. Studies have shown that sleep deprivation increases the brain's production of the hormone *ghrelin*—which tells you to keep eating—and reduce the production of the hormone *leptin*—which tells you you're full. If you don't get enough sleep, you eat more.

Blue light inhibits the brain's production of the hormone *melatonin*, which helps you fall asleep. It interferes with your gut buddies and your circadian rhythm, which leads to aging. Televisions, cell phones, computers, electronic devices, and most energy-saving light bulbs emit blue light. To get adequate sleep, you can:

- ❏ Reduce your blue light exposure at night by turning off all electronic devices or activating the nighttime lighting mode in their settings.
- ❏ Get a pair of blue light–blocking glasses and wear them after the sun while you are at home reading, watching TV, or on your computer.
- ❏ Take time-released melatonin supplements to reset your sleep-wake cycle from jet lag or night-shift.
- ❏ Keep a consistent sleep/wake rhythm by going to bed at the same time each night. Make sure you sleep a full eight hours before you need to wake up. Sleeping in on the weekend doesn't make up for time lost during the week.

Step 2: Kiss and Connect

Research shows that most centenarians have a strong social and spiritual support system. The Seventh-Day Adventists of Loma Linda live within a tight-knit community that provides both practical and spiritual support to all its members. Having a social network that goes beyond the immediate family has a dramatic impact on health and longevity. That may be why people see their health decline as soon as they retire. They lack their daily workplace social structure and become isolated, which ages them. In our culture, older folks tend to become isolated and depressed. As a result, we are seeing an epidemic of loneliness that coincides with our decreasing life and health spans.

Build your social network by joining a group—any group—whether it's a book club or a workout group. Volunteer at local organizations and pursue a new bobby. Purposeful living leads to improved social connections and a sense of belonging, two essential components in extending your life and health spans.

Online Video

1. Jog In Place (https://youtu.be/vrUA2dQk714)

2. How to Do Crunches (https://youtu.be/Xyd_fa5-zoEU)

3. How to Do a Proper Plank (https://youtu.be/B296mZDhrP4)

4. How to Do Squats for Beginners (https://youtu.be/otzWCWpuW-A)

5. High Intensity Interval Training Workout with No Equipment (https://youtu.be/_9Wls5hni0E)

6. How Sauna Use May Boost Longevity (https://youtu.be/eWKBsh7YTXQ)

7. The benefits of a good night's sleep (https://youtu.be/gedoSfZvBgE)

8. Sleep deprivation linked to an increase in Alzheimer's protein (https://youtu.be/FmDE8cJmf4s)

9. The unsung longevity factor of social connection (https://youtu.be/zXIBNFSkP0E)

Chapter 11
Longevity Paradox Supplement Recommendations

M any of the supplements that follow can enhance the results of the *Longevity Paradox* program. But they are not shortcuts. The first two—vitamin D_3 and the B vitamins—are essential for everyone.

Vitamin D_3

Most people have low levels of vitamin D_3. If you are just beginning this program, take 5,000 IUs of vitamin D_3 daily. For autoimmune diseases, start with 10,000 a day.

B Vitamins

Your gut buddies produce most of the B vitamins. If bad bugs control your gut, you're likely to be deficient in both methylfolate (folate acid) and methylcobalamin (Vitamin B_{12}). Many people have one or more mutations of the methylenetetrahydrofolate reductase (MTHFR) genes, which limits their ability to make the active forms of both vitamins. Since you have a 50-percent chance of carrying one or more of these single or double mutations, take a 1000 mcg methylfolate tablet and a 1000 to 5000 mcg methyl B_{12} each day to bypass the genetic mutation.

Polyphenols

Polyphenols are the most important class of plant phytochemicals missing from your diet. Plants concentrate these compounds in their fruits and leaves to resist insects and protect against solar radiation, so polyphenols provide you with a host of beneficial effects when metabolized by your gut bacteria. The leaves of a plant have more polyphenols than the fruit does. That's why olive leaf extract provides more of the benefits associated with olive oil. They can prevent atherosclerosis and dilate your blood vessels.

Polyphenols in supplement form include grape seed extract, pine tree bark extract (sometimes marketed as pycnogenol), and resveratrol, a polyphenol in red wine. Suggested dosages are 100 mg of both grape seed extract and resveratrol, and 25 to 100 mg of pine-tree bark extract a day. Other additions are green tea extract, berberine, cocoa powder, cinnamon, mulberry, and pomegranate.

Green Plant Phytochemicals

The phytochemicals in spinach reduce hunger for simple sugars and fats. Spinach extract is available in 500 mg capsules. Take two per day. Modified citrus pectin reduces myocardial and kidney stress. It comes as a powder or in 500 mg capsules. Take two capsules or one scoop per day.

Prebiotics

Probiotics are the bugs that live in and on you. Prebiotics are food for the probiotics to survive and grow. Prebiotics feed the good guys and starve the bad guys. Many of the compounds used for treating constipation, such as psyllium powder or husks, are food for your gut buddies; this makes them grow and multiply, accounting for that bigger bowel movement. The bad bugs in your gut can't eat psyllium husks and other fibers, so prebiotics feed the good guys and starve the bad guys.

One of the best prebiotics is inulin, a FOS. A mother's milk contains other important prebiotics known as galacto oligosaccharides (GOS), which feed the gut bugs of newborns. GundryMD PrebioThrive combines five prebiotics, including FOS and GOS, in a powder you mix with water and drink daily.

Lectin Blockers

GundryMD Lectin Shield combines nine ingredients to absorb or block lectins from reaching your gut wall. Take two capsules before a suspected meal.

Alternatively, you can take glucosamine and methylsulfonylmethane (MSM) in tablet form, which can also bind lectins. Products such as Osteo Bi-Flex and Move Free are available at Costco and other larger retailers. Also consider taking D-mannose, which is also in the Lectin Shield, in a dose of 500 milligrams twice a day, particularly if you are prone to urinary tract infections.

Sugar Defense

GundryMD Glucose Defense combines chromium, zinc, selenium, cinnamon bark extract, berberine, turmeric extract, and black pepper extract. You can take two capsules twice a day to change how your body and insulin handle the sugars you eat.

Costco sells a wonderful product called CinSulin, which combines chromium and cinnamon. Take two capsules a day. Combine this with

30 milligrams of zinc once a day, 150 micrograms of selenium a day, 250 milligrams of berberine twice a day, and 200 milligrams of turmeric extract a day.

Costco also offers an excellent turmeric supplement made by Youtheory. Take two of those a day. Because turmeric is so poorly absorbed, very little reaches your bloodstream. GundryMD offers a supplement called Biomax Curcumin, which is absorbed via a different mechanism and thus reaches much higher blood levels.

Long-Chain Omega-3s

Your brain is made up of 60 percent fat. Half of the fat in your brain is DHA, and the other half is arachidonic acid (AA)—great sources of which are egg yolks and shellfish. Studies have shown that people with the highest levels of omega-3 fats in their blood have a better memory and a bigger brain than people with the lowest levels. Fish oil also helps repair your gut wall and keeps those nasty LPSs from getting across your gut border.

Most people are deficient in omega-3 fatty acids EPA and DHA. People who have sufficient levels of these brain-boosting fats without taking supplements eat sardines or herring on a daily basis.

Take a fish oil and try to get 1000 mg of DHA per day. Look under "ingredients" to find the DHA content per capsule or teaspoon. Calculate how many capsules or teaspoons will get you at or above 1,000 milligrams of DHA per day.

Choose molecularly distilled fish oil. There are several good national brands available at Costco. GundryMD has an omega-3 supplement called Omega Advanced which combines omega-3 DHA with rosemary extract. A good-quality algae-derived DHA is also available for vegans.

Mitochondrial Boosters

The compounds that protect and stimulate mitochondria include:

- ❏ N-acetyl L-cysteine (NAC), 500 milligrams;
- ❏ Gynostemma extract, 450 milligrams;
- ❏ Shilajit, 300 milligrams;
- ❏ Reduced or L-glutathione, 150 milligrams;
- ❏ Pau d'arco, 50 milligrams;
- ❏ Pyrroloquinoline quinone (PQQ), 20 milligrams; and
- ❏ Nicotinamide adenine dinucleotide, reduced (NADH), 10 milligrams.

Supplements available to boost your nicotinamide adenine dinucleotide and oxidized (NAD+) levels include nicotinamide riboside and nicotinamide mononucleotide. These compounds activate the SIRT1 gene, which suppresses mTOR and, therefore, helps you live better and longer.

Supplementation During Rapid Weight Loss or Fasting

During an intermittent fast process, your body releases heavy metals and other toxins from your fat cells. Our body has a very poor ability to handle these toxins. So aim at losing no more than 50 pounds a year, or 12.5 pounds in three months. During fasting, consider supplementing with milk thistle, D-limonene, dandelion, N-acetylcysteine, activated charcoal, and chlorella.

Online Videos

1. Vitamin D: The Miracle Supplement (https://youtu.be/NXeqjUeqGhE)

2. Benefits Of B Vitamins (https://youtu.be/Uazyjv5QSBs)

3. "Top 10 Supplements for Longevity" by Dr. Zoltan P. Rona, MD (https://youtu.be/F5INW8Avv7U)

4. Dr. Mercola's "Core Five" Health Supplements (https://youtu.be/UYB_qTcT-hM)

5. Prebiotics: What they are and how to eat more (https://youtu.be/fAfBFpehGxg)

Index

About the Author

Lee Tang is a retired executive of a major global insurance company. Prior to his retirement, he has worked as an actuary, a risk officer, and a chief financial officer for several major insurance organizations in the United States, Canada, and Taiwan.

Plea from the Author

Hey, Reader. So you got to the end of my book. I hope that means you enjoyed it. Whether or not you did, I would just like to thank you for giving me your valuable time to entertain you. I am blessed to have such a fulfilling job, but I have that job only because of people like you; people kind enough to give my books a chance and spend their hard-earned money buying them. For that, I am eternally grateful.

If you would like to discover more about my other books then please visit my website for full details. You can find it at https://lmt-press.wordpress.com.

Also feel free to contact me by email (leetang888@gmail.com), as I would love to hear from you.

If you enjoyed this book and would like to help, then you could think about leaving a review—even if it's only a line or two—on your favorite bookstore, Goodreads, or other sites; and talk about the book with your friends. The most important part of how well a book sells is how many positive reviews it has, so if you leave me one then you are directly helping me to continue this journey as a full-time writer. Thanks in advance to anyone who does. It means a lot.

Lee Tang

Also by Lee Tang

Standalones

Dual Momentum Trend Trading: *How to Avoid Costly Trading Mistakes and Make More Money in the Stock, ETF, Futures and Forex Markets with This Simple and Reliable Swing Trading Strategy.*

Canada's Public Pension System Made Simple: *The Secrets To Maximizing Your Retirement Income From Government Pensions*

Summary & Study Guide Series

1. **Summary & Study Guide - Brain Maker:** *The Power of Gut Microbes to Heal and Protect Your Brain-Including Diet Cheat Sheet*
2. **Summary & Study Guide - The Gene:** *An Intimate History*
3. **Summary & Study Guide - The Emperor of All Maladies:** *A Biography of Cancer*
4. **Summary & Study Guide - NeuroTribes:** *The Legacy of Autism*
5. **Summary & Study Guide - Brain Storms:** *The Race to Unlock the Secrets of Parkinson's Disease*
6. **Summary & Study Guide - The End of Diabetes:** *The Eat to Live Plan to Prevent and Reverse Diabetes-Including Diet Cheat Sheet*
7. **Summary & Study Guide - The End of Heart Disease:** *The Eat to Live Plan to Prevent and Reverse Heart Disease-Including Diet Cheat Sheet*
8. **Summary & Study Guide - ADHD Nation:** *Anatomy of An Epidemic - Attention-Deficit/Hyperactivity Disorder*
9. **Summary & Study Guide - The Obesity Code:** *Unlocking the Secrets of Weight Loss*
10. **Summary & Study Guide - How Not to Die:** *Discover the Foods Scientifically Proven to Prevent and Reverse Disease*

For a complete list of books by Lee Tang and information about the author, visit *https://lmtpress.wordpress.com.*

CPSIA information can be obtained
at www.ICGtesting.com
Printed in the USA
BVHW041349060819
555199BV00015B/849/P